An Englishman's Journey along
America's Eastern Waterways

Tuesday July 12.

Stile very unwell, but induced to visit
the village 2½ miles distant to deliver an
evening lecture. had a large and an
attentive cong[n] and great anxiety express[d]
that my services should be repeated.

In the morning of this day visited
several individuals, and found them all
liberally inclined

Wednesday, July 13th. Left Pittsford for
Rochester, a busy town on the great
Erie canal – a pop[n] of 11.000 – and 16
years since there was not one house o[n]
the site of this now flourish[g] town. –

There is an abundance of water
power here, the Genesee, a considerable
river, having a considerable fall. –
on the N.E of the town, one of these
cataracts assumes an appearance of the
sublime. The whole body of the river
falls 96 feet in one unbroken sheet, over
a ledge of rocks stretching across the river. a
waterfall however looks sadly out of place
in the midst of a populous town.

# An Englishman's Journey along America's Eastern Waterways

## The 1831 Illustrated Journal of Herbert Holtham's Travels

Edited by
Seymour I. Schwartz

Rochester Museum & Science Center
and the
University of Rochester Press

First published 2000
by the Rochester Museum & Science Center
and the University of Rochester Press

The University of Rochester Press is an imprint of Boydell & Brewer, Inc.
668 Mount Hope Avenue, Rochester, NY 14620, USA
and of Boydell & Brewer, Ltd.
P.O. Box 9, Woodbridge, Suffolk 1P12 3DF, UK

ISBN 1–58046–079–8

**Library of Congress Cataloging-in-Publication Data**
Holtham, Herbert.
 An Englishman's journey along America's eastern waterways : the 1831
illustrated journal of Herbert Holtham's travels / edited by Seymour I. Schwartz.
  p. cm. illus. map
ISBN 1–58046–079–8 (alk. paper)
 1. Northeastern States—Description and travel. 2. Canada, Eastern—
Description and travel. 3. Northeastern States—Pictorial works. 4. Canada,
Eastern—Pictorial works. 5. Holtham, Herbert—Diaries. 6. Holtham,
Herbert—Journeys—Northeastern States. 7. Holtham, Herbert—Journeys—
Canada, Eastern. 8. Waterways—Northeastern States— History—19th century. 9.
Waterways—Canada, Eastern—History—19th century. 10. Unitarian
churches—England—Clergy—Diaries. I. Title: 1831 illustrated journal of Herbert
Holtham's travels. II. Schwartz, Seymour I., 1928- III. Title.

F8.H65 2000
917.404'3—dc21
                                                      00–039227

**British Library Cataloguing-in-Publication Data**
A catalogue record for this item is available from the British Library.

Printed in the United States of America.
This publication is printed on acid-free paper.

# Contents

# Herbert Holtham's Drawings
(beginning on page 175)

1. Hudson River
2. Mount Auburn Cemetery
3. Easton
4. Baltimore
5. Saw Mill, Delaware
6. Delaware River
7. Philadelphia Water Works, Schuykill River
8. Independence Hall, Philadelphia, originally the State House, built 1732
9. Christ Church, Philadelphia
10. New York, Hudson River
11. Near Baltimore
12. Genesee [River], Rochester [with Aqueduct Bridge]
13. Genesee River in Rochester
14. Rochester
15. Lower Falls, Rochester
16. Middle Falls, Rochester
17. Rochester Tannery
18. Kempshall's Mills, Rochester
19. Baltimore & Ohio Railroad
20. Montreal
21. Burned Forest near Ottawa
22. British Fort at Niagara
23. Queenstown
24. Niagara River
25. Canadian Falls
26. American Fall
27. Capitol, Washington
28. Gerards Bank, Phila.
29. Albany
30. The Monument, Baltimore

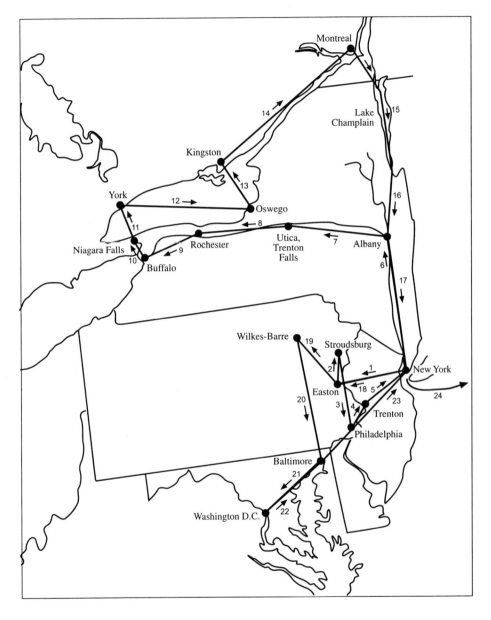

Map of Holtham's travels

# Preface

While I was in Chicago in September 1989 in quest of adding to a collection of maps focusing on North America before the nineteenth century, a dealer suggested that I consider an item that postdated the period of my interest but referred to the city and even the suburb in which I lived. A brief scanning of the manuscript, coupled with the excitement generated by the magnificent on-the-scene drawings, convinced me to purchase it immediately. Several readings of the text gave me even more pleasure, and the art became increasingly captivating. Research over the ensuing years revealed that this obscure work contained some of the earliest views of Rochester, several northeastern cities, the Erie Canal, and the recently incorporated Baltimore & Ohio Railroad.

The regional registry and church records of West Sussex, England, the area in which the journal's author resided, failed to uncover any pertinent information about him. The genealogy records available on the web site www.familysearch.org indicated that a Herbert Holtham married Sarah Brewer at St. Nicholas Parish, Brighton, Sussex, England on March 3, 1834.

I was committed to make this intriguing document with its delightful drawings available for others to enjoy, and, thereby, to share my love of American history, and perhaps reawaken an interest that lies dormant in many people.

## Acknowledgments

I would like to extend my sincere thanks to the Rochester Museum & Science Center and to the University of Rochester Press for their support in producing the book. I am also grateful to Jennifer Smith for the map of Holtham's journey and to Louise Goldberg for editorial help.

Seymour I. Schwartz
Rochester, New York
March 2000

# Introduction

The conclusion of the War of 1812 brought a lessening of the animosity between the United States and Great Britain. Trade between the two countries accelerated, and there was a marked increase in immigration, particularly from Scotland and Ireland. In the 1820s approximately 120,000 immigrants entered the United States from diverse countries of origin, and the number would explode to 540,000 in the 1830s. By that time twenty-four states had entered the Union, and the 1830 census counted more than twelve million people. Andrew Jackson was the president of the United States.

Changes in travel in the eastern part of the country occurred during the 1820s. In 1824, John Stevens's locomotive pulled a train for the first time at Hoboken, New Jersey. In 1827, the Baltimore & Ohio Railroad was incorporated as the first enterprise for commercial transport of people and freight. It began with horse-drawn carts on rail, and quickly converted to steam locomotive. In anticipation of an increase in travel, the Tremont Hotel opened in Boston in 1829 as the country's only first class hotel complete with interior bathrooms.

The first "road" to the interior, the Erie Canal, opened in 1825, providing egress from the Great Lakes to the Atlantic Ocean. It would eventually lead to the growth of many major cities; the first boom town was Rochester, New York, because of its location on the canal and a major river, the Genesee. The growth of the grain-milling industry was spurred by power provided by the ninety-foot waterfall in the heart of the city, and Rochester became known as the Flour City. Other canal communities like Utica, Fairport, Lockport, and Brockport also grew. In Manchester, about 20 miles from Rochester, the Church of Jesus Christ of Latter-Day Saints was organized in 1830. Pertinent to the following journal, in

1825 the American Unitarian Association was founded in Boston.

With a flowing readable script, Herbert Holtham, a well-to-do Unitarian minister with business interests—perhaps he was a draper—who resided in Brighton, England, recounts his travels in this journal. His voyage, from March 5th through September 20th, 1831, extended from his homeland across the Atlantic Ocean and through parts of the eastern United States and Canada. He paints a vivid picture not only of the cities and rural areas, but also of the people he met. He often stayed in people's homes, and recounts a number of conversations with those he met. At several points of call within the United States, he sermonized in Unitarian churches, and he recounts services he attended in other churches as well.

Besides describing many of his impressions in excellent prose, he shows his artistic talent by painting thirty scenes in the back of the journal; these are reproduced after the transcription of the text.

He begins with a narrative of his transatlantic sea voyage and a description of his fellow passengers. He made a brief stay in New York City, and while there, took a ferry to Hoboken, New Jersey. On the return crossing, he witnessed the rescue of a man who had fallen overboard. He describes New York City's steamboat traffic and general animation. Holtham then proceeded to Easton, Pennsylvania, and while in that community of 3000 people, he recounts the success story of a local miller. He continued to Stroudsburg by way of the beautiful Delaware Water Gap. Near that community, he participated in worship with members of the Hicksite sect, and watched militia training in the small town of Hambleton.

During a visit to the Pocono Mountains, he writes about a forest they passed that had been destroyed by fire. He also relates the temporary devastating effects of a rattlesnake bite in a boy who was successfully treated with tea from the bark of a white ash. He then traveled to Philadelphia, where he visited museums, the Pennsylvania Hospital, and the water works on the Schuykill River. While in Philadelphia he discusses the church-going and eating habits of Americans. As he crossed the Delaware River to Trenton, New Jersey, the number of jumping sturgeon he saw left a lasting impression. He returned to New York City by way of Princeton and New Brunswick.

His travels continued by steam boat up the Hudson River to Albany, a city of 24,000 inhabitants, and then west by packet boat on the Erie Canal, just 6 years after its completion. He stopped at Utica and visited Trenton Falls in the vicinity, which he described as an attraction for tourists. The boat passed the great salt works near Syracuse and proceeded to Pittsford, just east of Rochester. Holtham stayed in Pittsford for several days, and then spent a day in Rochester, a town of about 10,000 people. (He gives the number 11,000; the 1830 census lists 9,500 inhabitants.) He continued to Buffalo and Niagara Falls, which he describes in detail. After visiting York (Toronto), which at the time had a population of 5,000, he took a boat across Lake Ontario to Oswego, New York; he wrote movingly about witnessing a drowning as they crossed the lake.

Holtham then visited Kingston, the Thousand Islands, Montreal, and Lachine. Near Grenville, Ontario, the author met his brother, from whom he had been separated for fourteen years, and they traveled together for several days. They continued along the Ottawa River, where they watched the building of the Rideau Canal. After leaving his brother, Holtham left Canada, traveling via Lake Champlain to Albany, and then on to New York City, Trenton, and Philadelphia. An excursion to Wilkes Barre and the Wyoming Valley of Pennsylvania stimulated a recounting of the massacre that had occurred there and had been memorialized in verse.

After a brief trip to Harrisburg, Pennsylvania, he continued south to Maryland, the first slavery state he had visited, and he comments on the slavery question. Baltimore (population 80,000—the second largest city in the United States at the time) and Washington, D.C. (population 19,000) were his next stops. During part of the voyage in Maryland, the travelers rode in a horse-drawn stage on the tracks of the Baltimore and Ohio Railroad because the steam engine had broken down.

As the last leg of his travels, he went by boat from Baltimore via the Chesapeake-Delaware Canal to Philadelphia. He sailed for home from there on September 20th. After his arrival back home in England on October 14th, he penned some further reflections on America, its morals, its people, and his travels. The last entry is dated December 10.

## Description of the Journal

The journal is written in a book now measuring approximately 7¼ by 4¾ inches. The paper of the journal has watermarked writing lines; there is also a watermark date of 1828 throughout. There are several blank pages within the text of the journal; Holtham probably left room to add some reflections later. There are 3 blank leaves between the text and the drawings, and 54 blank leaves after the drawings.

The book was probably rebound after the journey, and is now bound in thin black leather over cardboard, with a flap covering the open edge. The strip into which the flap could be tucked is missing. The front cover has a small accordion-fold pouch into which other papers could be placed. The prayer by Holtham (transcribed on page 171) was found folded into this pouch. There are two leaves without the writing lines at both front and back of the book; it is on the first of these that Holtham wrote his name, address, and address in America, perhaps later. Thus page 1 of the journal (on the watermark-lined paper) is the entry for March 5, 1831.

# Editorial Practices

The transcripton retains the line breaks of the original.

The pagination of the text reproduces Holtham's pagination; page numbers he omitted have been added in brackets.

The transcription is as clear as possible:

Words crossed out in the journal are indicated by an overstrike: ~~the~~.

Words or letters added by the editor are included in square brackets []. In spite of old and/or inconsistent spelling, these bracket changes have been kept to a minimum.

Occasional illegible words are replaced by [*illegible*].

The dashes so prevalent throughout Holtham's text are of varying lengths and at varying distances from the preceding words or punctuation. These have been made consistent in both length and distance.

Holtham's use of capital letters is not always obvious from his penmanship; the editor admits that his interpretation of these letters may not always agree with someone else's.

In the picture captions, commas have been added for clarification and capitalization has been standardized.

Seymour I. Schwartz
Rochester, New York
March 2000

Herbert Holtham
42 East St.
Brighton
England

Address in America
Co Mr. W. Goodacre
34 Park
New York

Saturday Mch. 5th. 1831

I am now about to undertake an affair
the duties of which will be very different from
those which have hitherto been connected with
my life: clouds and darkness it is true are
gathered round the future o̷f̷ m̷y̷ l̷i̷f̷e̷, but yet
though I leave the comforts of a home, and the
certain provision which was offered for my
acceptance, I have every reason to believe
that my change of situation will be for the better.
Under circumstances like these, when my
mind is of course in a somewhat more serious
mood than usual, I feel anxious to strengthen
my confidence in the wisdom o̷f̷ and goodness of
that Divine Being who has hitherto been my
Father and my Friend, and to bind around my
heart the solemn yet consoling truth, that <u>all</u>
<u>his</u> <u>ways</u>, though they sometimes appear to us,
painful and useless are ever the <u>kindest</u>, the
<u>wisest</u> and the <u>best</u>. Of this I may be certain,
that under the government of an infinitely
wise and benevolent God, my happiness the
great end of my existence, is within mine own

[2]

power, while reason and revelation combine to
convince me that virtue and Piety present the
most certain of attaining to it: Be it my
endeavour to cultivate a state of mind and
heart favorable to their development, and
may.the God whom I seek to serve and to
know and love aid me in the holy work.

If prosperity and happiness should be
my portion may I enjoy with moderation
the temporal good allotted to me, ever remem-
bering that prosperity is a more dangerous
trial than adversity, and if tribulation and
disappointment should cross me, be it mine
to have resigned to the Divine will, and to
seek in the consciousness of present virtue
and the prospect of future blessedness that highest good, of which neither life nor death can
deprive me. —

Be it my endeavour to cultivate
the much neglected duty of morning and every
prayer and praise to the Almighty, so that
if erring nature should sometimes lead me to
wander <u>far</u>, at least I may not wander long
from goodness and from God.

It will be useful for me to lay down some plan of enquiries to be made and information to be gained respecting America; the growth of this empire presents a spectacle and a lesson which the world has never before seen, differing as its acknowledged principles do from other nations in political social moral and religious respects, it presents an interesting field for speculation. The following are subjects which deserve to be well considered.

1 Constitution
2 Internal regulations
3 Productions
4 Commerce
5 Population
6 { Moral state of
    { Society
7 Religion
8 Influence in the world
9 Connexion with England
10 Emigration

4

Sunday Mch. 6th.

In the acquisition of new friends
and new ideas, let me not forget those with
whom I have hitherto been connected by the ties
of friendship and of kindred: independent of the
mere pleasure connected with the remembrances
of "auld lang syne", the memory of the past is
truly valuable, from the tendency which it has
to spiritualize the mind and to develop extended
powers of perception. We all live too much for
the present, and require continually to be reminded
that there are higher objects before us which can
only be attained by governing the present from
a deep conviction of how much our future destiny
is connected with it, and I do not know a more
certain means of strengthening this conviction, than
by experiencing how forcibly the past affects the present.
Amongst those whom I wish to remember and
correspond with I may mark the following

| Sister Mary | I. Rogers |
| "   Mili | B. Evans |
|      Nieces | G. Cooper |
| W. Hack | W. Molleson |
| C. Cooper | S. Francis senr. & junr. |

R. Aspband          W. Cubley
G. Beringham
P. Taylor
Courtauld & Co
Mrs. Harwood
J. Martin
__ Stevens
W. Hussey
J. Browne
__ Martin
__ Wallace

     It has been a matter of great surprize
to me that I should feel such an utter indifference at
leaving my native country — no "last fond lingering looks"
have mine eyes taken of the cliffs of old England, no sentimen-
tal tears have they shed. I am really almost ashamed of
my want of feeling, and my perfect composure is ~~really~~
quite provoking. How different now from what it
would have been a few years since, and what is it that
has made such an alteration? but this would be too
long an enquiry for the present moment.

     The following is a list of letters in my
of introduction or to send. —
          P.O

To J. Vaughan Esq. Philadelphia
      from R. Goodacre
To Dr. Meuse Philadeplhia
      from R. Goodacre
To Richard Peters Esq. Philadelphia
      from R. Goodacre
To Benjamin Grutt Esq                    of Do.
      from P. A. Tayler
To Mr. Richard Allen                     of Do.
      from P. A. Tayler
To Mr. James Taylor                      of Do.
      from Revd. R. Aspland
To John Warder Mercht.                   of Do.
      from Mary Capper
To __ Cox Esqr. —                        of Do.
      from P. A. Taylor
To Cadbury —                             of Do.
      from E. Pryan
To __ Wymbs Esqr.   New York
      from Stuart Hargraves
To Mr. Stephen Rowland   Albany
      from Rowland

To Mr. Thos. Agate  Mount Pleasant
         from Jas. Browne
To Mr. Thos. Billingshurst  Pitsford
         from Jas. Browne
To __ Do.  Do.  Do.
         from . . . . . . . . .
To Mr. Thomas Oakenden Pittsford
         from . . . . . . . . . .


All letters and papers connected with Mrs. H.[']s
estate to be kept separately. —


Mch. 3  Left London on thursday being towed to
Gravesend — nothing particular occurred: there are
9 cabin and about 50 steerage passengers
Mch. 4  sailed only a few miles wind being
contrary — at night one of the men fell from
the main yard on the deck — much hurt but
likely to recover.
Mch. 5       reached Margate — wind contrary
some of the passengers ill, obliged to anchor
in the roads until this disagreable S.W has
blown over.

[8]
March 6th.
              The felicity of lying at anchor
all day fell to our portion. Being Sunday
I of course employed part of the day in reading and meditation
Mch. 7th.  Wind still contrary but in the
afternoon a favorable breeze sprung up which carries
us to Dungeness point.
Mch. 8.          A fine steady breeze from SSW,
past Beachy Head at 8 AM. too misty however
to perceive its grandeur — away — away 10 knots
per hour a passing sigh to my friends at East-
Dean and in another hour a telescope discovered
Brighton at about 10 miles distance, and here
I thought of home and those who had made home
dear to me, another gaze another wish, another
prayer and I lost sight of a place where I
had spent many an happy hour. — at 2 we
saw the Isle of Wight at 3 we anchored 4 m.
off Portsmouth and after dinner we took a boat
to visit the celebrated place. I found it very
dull and very dirty. Whilst I was gone to
Portsea, a curious occurrence took place — a
Frenchman (cabin passenger) was seized by the

Police having robbed his employer the Comte de
Villele of about 1000£ sterling. It was fortunate
that he was not apprehended on board as loaded pistols
were found under the pillow of his cot. — Our return
at 7 P.M. was the most wretched journey I ever
experienced wet and so stormy that we were two hours
making the vessell. —

Mch. 9th.  The wind contrary but a glorious day
visited the Isle of Wight in the afternoon and spent
two hours at Ryde — what a charming spot, oh for
500£ per annum and . . . . . . to make me happy in such a place. The wind has veered to a fa
vourable point and we shall be off with daylight. —

Mch. 10  Many a slip between the cup and the
lip, the wind has returned to an adverse
quarter, and we are still anchored where we
were yesterday.

Mch. 11 — Another day of the same cast.

Mch. 12 — The wind still the same quarter
but augmented to a hurricane — it is fortunate
that we are not at sea, for it would run
mountains high, and render everything
very uncomfortable. —

10

Mch 13th. Sunday

Another day of storm and darkness,
impossible to sail as the sea would run very
high in the channel: nevermind I shall have
more leisure to think, and to do so is a duty
which ought to be discharged upon this, perhaps
more than any other day. I have often thought
what an advantage to is in many respects to
possess such a day as the Sabbath, a cessation
from corporal and intellectual labour. By reposing from bodily labour, the frame has time and
opportunity to recover from the fatigues and to
replace the exhausted energies of the past week,
while the mind released from the task of requiring
lessons of worldly wisdom, is gently guided into the
region of moral and religious contemplation, where
as the soul wanders by the still waters of peace
and truth, every wild passion is hushed and every
unholy thought is banished far away. This is the
time for communion with God and renewing
of his holy spirit, for meditation upon Jesus
and the heavenly truths he lived and died to
teach. Oh my soul remember the eternity which
is before Thee.

Mch. 14th. Monday

      The wind in the same quarter — as I could
only complain if I were to write. it will doubtless be the
wiser plan to shut the book. — It will not however
(as I have nothing better to do) be useless to remind
myself, that I find myself to have indulged too much
in desultory reading, and conversations in which I
have recently taken a part, prove to me the want
of some systematic method of acquiring information.
It would be better doubtless to epitomize part of the books
which I read, and in so doing not only concentrate
the facts which they contain, but impress their remembrance more deeply upon my mind.

Mch. 15  Tuesday.  No variation

  "  16  Wednesday.   Do. Do.

  "  17  Thursday     Do. Do.

  "  18  Friday. Thank God at last
a gentle N.W has sprung up and at 2 PM we
weighed at anchor and by midnight saw the
light at Portland point.

Mch. 19.  Saturday  little wind but reach
Start Point in the evening.

Mch. 20.  Start Point still in view and
a perfect calm. Never have I seen the

12

ocean look more beautiful. There is not
a wave, nay scarce the smallest ripple upon
the vast expanse, and I could almost fancy it
to be the Sabbath of nature. It is in the midst
of scenes so calm so beautiful that a sense of the
Divine Being i̶s̶ e̶v̶e̶r̶ p̶r̶e̶s̶e̶n̶t̶ comes home to the
innermost depths of the soul. The solemn conviction that God is, gathers depths and intensity from
the calm beatitude which pervades his mighty
works: we feel after him and we find him in
the creation which bears witness of his glory.
Mch. 21 — Monday — Still at Start Point.
What a misnomer! we appear as if we should
never start from it
Mch. 22.  An easterly breeze is sprung up
before the wind 8 knots all day.
Mch. 23  Wednesday — No variation
Mch. 24  Thursday —     Do.
Mch. 25  Friday, light contrary winds
Mch. 26  Saturday — a calm — longitude 23 20
   "   27  Sunday — a fine North East breeze
This day I calculated the time when the new
Road chapel commences service, and endea
voured to bring my own mind to a state of

worship.

   How pure, how precious — how holy and how happy are the feelings we experience when communing with our Maker, and how consoling it is to reflect, that weak and erring as we are, the Divine Being permits and encourages us us to approach the "habitations of his Holiness", and to drink deep of the living waters which gush from the footsteps of His Throne.

Mch. 28 Monday. A fine South West breeze going 9 knots all day — Saw a whale

Mch. 29. Tuesday. Awoke at 7 AM by a heavy squall striking the vessel. by 9 A.M. the wind increased to a gale nearly a hurricane from the N.W. The vessell rode gallantly over and occasionally thro' the seas. I had formed great expectations of the sublimity of such a scene nor was I disappointed, and not being troubled with sickness I really enjoyed its grandeur. The gale lessened gradually and we continued within a point of our course at 6 Knots all night at 12 noon in Longitude 35. 36. lat 65.2. not quite half distance. This on Wednesday.

[14]

Mch. 31. Thursday.  A fine wind
from N.E. 8 Knots — longitude 39.10
Apl. 1. Friday.  fine breeze from the NE
have this day (24 H.) run 202 miles — we are
in longitude 44.00. lat. 43.40
Apl. 2  Saturday - a light breeze.
Apl. 3  Sunday.  a light N. but dull and
hazy as is always upon or near the Banks
of Newfoundland. Having taken up the 1
vol. of "Devereux", I could not bear to leave
it unfinished — the more serious duties of the
day were, in a great measure unattended to.
Devereux is a singular and a powerful work
it contains a great deal of intellectual and
some moral development —
Apl. 4  Monday.  Found that we had passed
over the Banks during the night and wer
in longitude 51.40. The weather still
hazy and unpleasant but a favourable breeze.
I will seize this opportunity of noting down
my fellow passengers in the cabin 1st Genl
Wavell, a middle aged and a very small man
but who, according to his own act. has shot
more, seen more variety, has more titles

and more remarkably clever friends, and is
altogether a more important personage than
any other man in creation; a dimutive dimin-
ution of humanity, he is full of conceit and self
importance, and though weighing at the very utmost
7 stone, has the effrontery to stretch out his puny
arm, and exclaim as he challenges the examination
of his smiling audience "There's muscle". This individual is notwithstanding very clever and really
possesses a great variety of information. 2ndly
Mr. Turner of New York, Editor of an old Tory Paper
in that city, an old Americain, fervently but quietly
attached to his country and its institutions, but unas-
suming and respectable. 3 Mr. Turner Junr
a thorough going yankee who can see no good, no
beauty out of the U.S. stop I am wrong, he has
found something good and beautiful in an English
wife whom he is taking over and who as No.4
is a very good sort of woman and that's all
5 Mr. Green, a young intelligent and pleasing
American merchant, without prejudice, good humours
and fun. He has shown good sense in selecting
for a wife 6. Mrs. Green, Francaize, young
pretty, full of spirits and perfectly "ladylike"

16

7 Mr. Vaughan, an Irishman a thorough Irishman, and consequently pleasing
8 Mr. Brooman — a young Englishman of
good mercantile connexions, but lamentably
deficient in most things which can ~~alone~~ render
a man truly valuable. There is a superficial
power of pleasing which respectability of station
has conferred upon him, <u>au fond</u> he is without
heart, without energy, without soul education or
religion — 9 Cap. Sebor the commander of the
vessel, enough of the gentleman to prevent him
from being a brute, and enough of a seaman
to prevent him from being quite a gentleman.
Apl. 5 Tuesday — light breeze from SW
with a shoal of porpoises in the lee beam.
Apl. 6 Wednesday, another north wester
but not quite so violent as the last.
Apl. 7 Thursday. a light S.W. veered to W
in the night and blew very hard.
Apl. 8 Friday — W continued to blow, the
sea running exceedingly high; the appearance
at night was magnificent; the surf assumg.
a phosphorescent and brilliant appearance,
which contrasted with the dark mass of

waters presented a brilliant and singular
spectacle — utterly impossible to sleep at night
from the rolling and pitching of the vessel.
Apl. 9 Saturday. Wind rather moderated
  " 10 Sunday — wind and sea gradually
sinking  a S. breeze sprung up at night
and carried us on 7 Knots an hour.
Apl. 11 — Monday. no change
  " 12 Tuesday. A tremendous gale from
the S.W. changing at last to a regular
north wester.
Apl. 13. Wednesday. the gale gradually
dying away and the wind from the west
about 160 miles from New York.
Apl. 14. Thursday. a fine day and favourable breeze.
Apl. 15 Friday. Enjoyed at last the prospect of land: Long Island being about 10 m.
distant, but unfortunately a fog coming were
obliged to bear off all night.
Apl. 16. Saturday. A strong breeze and heavy
fog. obliged to tack and heave the lead continually — our situation very dangerous
Apl. 17. Sunday. the weather cleared

[18]

and at 6 P.M. we had the pleasure of
seeing L. Island once more and in another
hour the lights of "Never Sink" were visible;
stood on for the harbour and procured a pilot
but anchored outside the harbour: The scene
was beyond anything beautiful and romantic.
Apl. 18 Monday. Made signals for a steamboat
to take us in tow, and at length entered the harbour
the scenery of which is exquisitely beautiful, and
presents a coup d'œil not easily to be forgotten.
The day was fine & calm and I perhaps enjoyed the scenery more for having been so long deprived of the
prospect of anything but sea and sky; we passed Staten
Island were examined by the Doctor, and after passing
the batteries and the small island in the river were
at last anchored in the quay. We immediately left
the vessell, and entered at once into this first city
of the New world. I shall take a future opportunity of describing it, and of making a few comments upon the people and manners. We put
up at the Americain Hotel, where we met with
a luxurious reception.
Apl. 19 Tuesday, Employed in rambling over
the city, and in procuring our baggage from

the vessell. In order to do this it is
necessary to procure a permit from the custom
House where you are obliged to swear that your
baggage contains nothing but what is bona fide
for your personal use, and one of the officers on
board upon this being presented examines your
baggage and allows it to pass. We left the
A. Hotel and took up our quarters at a boarding
house, the terms of which were 5 dollars per week
for which we were found in breakfast, dinner,
tea, bed and a plentiful supply of dirt and impu-
dence. Poor Vaughan was sadly put out of his
way by the inconveniences of the place, and I
although not over particular, could not avoid con-
trasting my present with my past abode, and
turned, oh how fondly, turned to my own country &
my own home, and the dear members of my that
home's fireside, as to that, for the loss of which nothing
in America could fully compensate.
Apl. 20  Wednesday — Passed over the north river to
Brooklyn, a town connected with N.Y. and to and from
which steam boats pass every five minutes.
Endeavord. to procure other lodgings, but the Town
completely full of strangers.

Apl. 21. Thursday — a fine & pleasant
day employed in perambulating the city.
Apl. 22 Friday. — At home with the pleasant prospect of a public execution on a
small island opposite the windows of my apartment
the criminal is a notorious pilate, who in the
space of a few years has been instrumental in
the death of more than 400 individuals. Wrote
my first letters to sisters and Mrs. H[arwoo]d and
shall send them by the "Sylvanus Jenkins" which
sails on the 26th. Mili's letters to be addressed
to the same address as before, Mrs H. to the Post office
Philadelphia — Drank tea with Wm. Goodacre who
is just married, a pleasant evening and kind
reception. A friend of his in the post office will forward my letters until 1st July to Philadelphia.
Apl. 23. Saturday — Called on Mr. Greene 6
Hammersley Street, accompan[ie]d Mr. Vaughan in
a perambulation through the town, and an examination of some of the steamboats. There are a
great number of these floating palaces between
N.Y. and Albany which is situated 150 miles up the
Hudson, this distance they perform in 10 hours
the passage being $2.

In the afternoon took the ferry to Hoboken, a picturesque village on the Hudson opposite
to N.Y. To me who for years have dwelt amidst
the barren splendour of Brighton, and for two months
have sailed upon the dreary sea, the sight of the
rural beauties of this village and neighbourhood were
truly refreshing and delightful, and true to custom.
I breathed many a wish for love and a cottage on
each beautiful site that I passed by. Alas it is not
to be.     I met here for the first time
the Americain custom of the quantity of spirits,
when you call for refreshment, being left entirely to
the ¢h̸a̸r̸g̸e̸ discretion of the drinker, the bottle being
placed before him. After spending an agreable evening
in this enchanting place, we returned by ferry
boat, when just before arriving at our port, we
were alarmed by the cry of "man overboard" — and a
drunken fellow <u>had</u> fallen in the river, but very
fortunately rose again and swam like a duck
to the pier where he was hauled up, to both his and
our great satisfaction.  A few days since while
passing along the wharf, I happened to cast my
eye into a kind of cellar, attached to a tavern, and
such a revolting spectacle I never before beheld.

22

The long low cavern was full of blacks,
many of whom were in the state of absolute drunkenness, all more or less intoxicated, the smoke of
tobacco, the reeking breath of such a number, the
dismal light of the place, just sufficient to show its
horrors, ḏẇǿḵǿ the infernal noise of jabber and
imprecation, presented a scene more replete with
every thing that can disquiet, than I have ever
elsewhere seen. The authorities of the city have found
out an admirable plan for lessening the number of
public exhibitions of drunkeness. Every carrier
and of this useful class there are no less in this
busy place than 1400 each with a horse and cart
can claim upon delivering an intoxicated subject
at Bredewell 3/4 of a dollar [—] a sum which en-
sures their vigilance, and produces a check upon
this disquieting vice, which might be advantageously pursued elsewhere. Let it be understood
that I think that there is not so great a proportion of drunkenness here as in England, a
fact which settles at once the question of a low
price for spirits, nor do I think that I have seen
an individual intoxicated in the street excepting
the crew or passengers of our own vessell.

Apl. 24 Sunday. Attended Divine wors-
hip at the Chamber Street Church, (for all places
of worship are called churches in America,) where
Mr. Ware delivered an excellent discourse to a
congregation which for numbers and respectability actually surprized me. After service introduced myself to Mr. W. and was kindly welcome[d]
as an English Unitarian. The evening was spent
in a ramble over the New Jersey shore, round
to Hoboken. The face of the country in that
quarter varies considerably, but the soil appears remarkable fertile, the evening calm
and beautiful.
Apl. 25. Monday. Examined some of the large
steamboats on the North or Hudson. There are
a great number of very fine ones, but the most
splendid amongst them is the North America
which for size and magnificence, surpasses ever-
y thing of the kind I ever met with. Its
length is 160 feet, and against wind and tide it
will sail at the rate of 16 miles per hour.
The evening was spent partly in writing &
partly in conversation with the two friends
Vaughan and Brooman from whom I

24

I was in the morning to part, after
having much enjoyed their company during
the voyage, and the week which I had remained in New York. This city, certainly
the capital of the United States, derives much
of its importance, from its commercial connexion with Europe, the number of vessels,
which in the year arrive from, or sail to,
all parts of the world being very large, and
though the vessells are not generally speaking of
so large a class, as those which fill the docks
at Liverpool, yet the yearly tonnage of the
port must be very great. It is also frequen-
ted at this season of the year by the country
buyers, who resort hither, as to the best supplied
market, from all quarters of the Union.
As far as regards commerce, the city bears
every mark of prosperity and increase, the
filling up of the streets with crowds of men, and
loads of merchandize, assures the spectator
that there is employment enough to occupy
the energies of thousands, and bales and casks
and all the cetera of commerce, too numerous
and bulky to be contained in the

warehouses of olden time.

There is an air of animation and
intellect about every one you meet, that immediately raises your opinion of the place,
and when to this we add, that the men dress
exceeding well and that the ladies are very
handsome and very tasty in their apparel
nay that many of them have l'air ["]tout
à fait distingué", who does not long to be
a dweller in this "city of the west".

It may give some idea of the mixed
nature of society in this place, when I state
that not more than one third of its inhabitants
are natives of it, the colored race form no
small portion of its dwellers, probably about
1/8, the Irish labourers &c are at least equal
in number, but between these two classes
the line of distinction appears to be carefully
observed, while here and there you meet with
a man, who from his powerful but rather gaunt
frame, and the peculiar cut of his visage would
be known for an Americain all the world over
but I shall have more to say of these gentry
hereafter. —

We are accustomed in Europe too much
to think that America is an empire of equals —
no idea can be more erroneous; there are
many classes and grades between all of whom there
are distinctions, and those two generally acknowledged and understood, and I think that even
here, the meanest kind of aristocracy, that of
riches, is regarded with a veneration not surpassed even if equalled in Europe, but I
am perhaps hasty in this remark, and a
longer acquaintance with, and a wider field
of observation upon the people, will perhaps
correct and alter my present crude notions
of them and their manners. —

Apl. 26        Chapter II

On the Tuesday morning I embarked on
a steamer and after sailing down the bay passed
up Staten Island sound, along the Raritan, the
banks of which are of a quiet character,
and landed at New Brunswick, from
where we took the stage to Easton a distance
of 45 miles. My "campagnons de voyage" were
very agreable, and as two ladies were amongst
the number, we contin[ue]d to pass a very

pleasant 9 hours of it, notwithstanding
a succession of jolts and concussions, which
was happily though unexpectedly upon my
part, unattended by dislocation or fracture,
but my companions were most of them, literal-
ly speaking <u>old stagers</u>, and took it all as a
matter of course. Upon understanding
that I was an "Inglisher" one of the old country, they all became much interested, and as
they, had never been out of the states, were
glad of any information that I could afford
them. I flatter myself that I was quite
a "lion" amongst them, at any rate I am
sure that I was pleased with them, and we
parted with friendly wishes, accompanied by
hearty invitations to come and spend a
few days with two of them. The route lay thro' New
Jersey up the Raritan, from New Brunswick
through Roundrook, Somerville, white House
Potters Town, at which latter place there
is a pretty waterfall with a mill seat, and
then over some very high and rocky country
to Easton. There are about here particularly many of the original forests, rem-

28

aining, and though none of them are of
great extent, I could not regard them, but with
a feeling of something like veneration; the trees
however in this part of the country do not appear to grow to a large size. We crossed
a great number of small and two larger streams
and at nine oclock in the evening reached
Easton, where I was glad to rest my weary
bones. The morning after
Wednesday 27th  was employed in the land office
and the afternoon in an excursion up the
Banks of the Delaware which is here about the
size of the Trent at Nottingham in England
I found some truly picturesque and sublime
scenery, and if I have time to visit the gap
in the mountain thro' which the Delaware runs
I am promised one of the finest spectacles in
America. Easton is situated upon the junction of the Lehigh and Delaware, the first
of which has derived much importance latterly
from being the means of conveying the coals
from the mountain lands. — The country about
is exceeding fertile, and the farmers are old —
established and rich. The town contains

about 3000 souls, and forms altogether an
interesting and a pretty object, amongst the high
and woody country by which it is overlooked.
Being in conversation with an intelligent hardy
looking man, he gave me a short history of his
life, as a proof he said that industry and persev-
everance always, in America at least met with
their reward. as illustrating American
"maniere de vivre" I give it in his own words.
My Father was an English emigrant, from what
part I do not know, my Mother was German.
He had been a labourer but took and cleared
a small farm where I was raised. At nine
years old I was put out a service, and saved
a little money — at twenty three I married, and
was employed in a saw and grist mill. I
there learned how to construct them, and in a
few more years having saved a few hundred
dollars altogether, I took a farm of seventy
five acres for which I was to pay a certain
sum, by instalments — I erected a mill and
the first year cut lumber enough to pay the
price of the farm.

In a few more years I had money to

spare, and having befriended an old hunter
in the neighbourhood, he came to me one day and said,
put your knapsack, Peters, on your back and
your gun over your shoulder, and come with
me, and I'll show I guess where to buy a bargain.
Knowing the man to be honest, I went with
him and in the centre of woods, which I had
always thought impenetrable, he showed me a
valley of 100 acres, which he said was every spring
with snow water enough to turn a mill all
summer — the proprieter lived at New York
To New York I went, purchased the land at
3. 4 & 5 dollars an acre, erected two mills and
am now worth 45000 thousand dollars.
Such is the history of this man & such are or
at least have been the facilities for doing well.
Thursday Apl. 28.  Wet all day, and spent the
afternoon in the City Hall where the assizes
were holding. I could not [help] being somewhat
amused with the republican tone of manners,
and although the general routine of a trial
is much the same as in England, yet I think
the proffessional gentlemen indulge themselves in a most unwarrantable degree

of verbosity; the summing of the Judge,
a gentleman of the name of Mallory, was
exceedingly clever and sensible. Most of the wit-
nesses were german, and an interpreter was
made use of. The number of Germans and
Dutch in this neighbourhood is very great, as
they form a large majority of the inhabitants.
Friday Apl. 29. took a horse and set
off for Stroudsburg, a small town on the
other side the blue mountains at the distance of 28 miles from Easton. The ride
to this place is one of the most beautiful
that can be imagined. There are two routes
to it from Easton, one through a pass in
the mountains called the Wind Gap, the
other through one named the Water Gap,
which latter one was chosen by me, as I
had been informed that the scenery there
was remarkably fine. Nor was I disappointed.      A reference to page 28 will
give an unworthy description of the first part
of my ride, let me however add, that the
country thro' which the pure spring like
water of the Delaware rolls, contains in

the first 10 miles almost every variety of
beauty, which nature can exhibit, the beautiful
river in the dell, the shore sometimes rocky and
precipitous, rich and luxuriant foliage every
where, green islands studding the blue water
and a thousand thousand songsters making
sweet melody around you. At the distance
of about 10 m. from Easton, you leave
the river, and wind along the bank of
a smaller stream, on which are several
saw mills, all of which seem busily employed.
and at about the distance of two miles I
was alarmed at the road diminishing to a
mere unworn path, at one corner of which
stood the ghost of a sign post, stretching forth
a solitary arm, which conveyed the very
interesting information, that this was the road
to "Shumans Mill"; as this was obviously,
bending in a different direction from the
course I wished to pursue, I looked around
for some time before I discovered that my
road lay <u>through</u>, not over a deep and
swift stream, which I had no sort of
wish to ford. I paused, make haste

over said my old acquaintance <u>hurry,</u>
you had better not attempt it said <u>Comfort</u>
when a stern voice from the iron lips of
Necessity exclaimed, You must go through it
there is no other way.   With a courage in-
spired by this disagreeable mandate, I went
in, and actually reached the other side with
out being drowned. After passing through
New Brunswick, I again approached the
Delaware, and could perceive at a weary distance the gap which formed one great object
of my journey, and the nearer approach
to it convinced me that my expectations
would be fully gratified. Within 1/2 a mile
of the pass, the banks of the river become
clothed with a great variety of trees, amongst
which the verdant laurel holds a conspicuous
place, but immed[iatel]y upon entering the gap
the scene becomes changed. The River which
is here perhaps 150 yards wide runs between
two abrupt and rocky mountains, which rise
on either side to the elevation of 1360 feet.
on the north side the masses of rock are
peculiarly grand, and upon the very summit

34

of this elevation, there may be seen
a considerable lake, about a mile and half
in length, and one mile in breadth, the
depths of which has not ever been fathomed,
but which furnish a safe and distant hab-
itation for every variety of fish. The banks
precipitous as they are, are clothed with the
richest foliage, and the old grey rocks themselves
bear on their tops and in their crevices the sombre
green of many a pine; but perhaps the most
interesting feature of this singular dell is the
profusion of springs and cascade, the streams
of which originate in the surrounding mountains, and whose living waters pour themselves
forth over the steep rocks or through the over-
hanging shrubbery, cheering the eye with their
bright sparkling, and making with their
murmurs sweetest melody. H̸o̸w̸ g̸r̸a̸n̸d̸ i̸s̸ t̸h̸e̸
The fish hawk sailing on its wide spread wing
between the mountains, and appearing to reign
the undisputed savage lord of the whole scene, added
yet more wildness and strangeness to a place,
the beauties of which I can never forget.
        After travelling about 4 miles thro'

a succession of similar scenery the road
turns off, and at the distance of 3 miles leads
you to Stroudsburg, where I took up my
quarters for the night.
Saturday Apl. 30.  Accompanied Mr. Morris
Robeson, in a journey through some of the
neighbouring woods, where he was cutting and
hauling timber, or as they elegantly paraphrase
it here lumber. The wood or rather forest
lay upon the top and side of a range of hills
running nearly parallel with the Katanning
or blue mountains, and as this was the first
aboriginal forest I had been in, I was of
course ready to remark its features; After
winding thro' a course, where an experienced
and discerning eye could now & then discover
something like a path, but where nothing
but American enterprize would undertake
to find a road, we heard the sound of the
heavy axe, and a loud[?] voice cheering the horses
in their work, and presently after joined the
men who were at work also. and I can most
conscientously assure you that their labours are
not of the lightest kind.   Independently of

of the immense masses of wood which the men
have to fell and the horses to draw, the huge
rocks and stumps which strew, nay form the
very groundwork of the forest, present obstacles
which to the eye of an Englishman who has
been accustomed to Macadamized roads, which
appear utterly insurmountable. As this part
of forest and is  not very often visited by fire
it has a healthy and pleasing and rather than
a desolate appearance; when I name however
that it is the resort of rattle snakes, pilots
bears deer panthers & wolves, you will readily
imagine that it is not quite a paradise.
In one direction, the road to Milford, you
pass 29 miles of forest without meeting a
single house. — Spent the evening with
Mr. R. a pleasant chat and a good cigar.
I met at the same house an old gentleman
an uncle of Mr. R. a quaker, facetious
and merry enough to be sure, but if I
laughed at his jokes, I am sure I wondered
at his being about to undertake a journy
to the western country, and to which,
although he must travel over 3000 miles

he looked forward with an indifference
absolutely astounding to an Islander like
me. The Americains, on their steamboats
in their stages, on horseback, or in their useful little waggons, travel almost any distance
apparently without any exertion, and consider
a journey of one or two thousand miles
as a mere matter of course.

Sunday Apl. 31 [i.e., May 1]. After breakfast concluded to
attend divine worship at Hicksite mee-
ting, the manners and principles of which
accorded so much with my own feeling, as to
secure my enjoyment in performing the act
of obedience and reverence towards my Maker.
It may be useful to state, that the Hicksites
as they are here termed, are that part of the
society, who have professed an attachment to
the principles advocated by the late Elias Hicks
and which from their republican spirit and
simplyfying tendency, cannot of course be expected to suit the aristocratic notions and orthodox
principles of the more starched elders of the society. Their principles are in the main
Unitarian, and they are careful to state that

38

these principles are derived from the
early friends Fox, Penn &c. — The meeting
was small and simple, but God requires not
a gorgeous temple and crowded assembly to
make worship acceptable, his holiest temple
is the contrite and obedient heart, and whenever
and wherever the prayer and praise of such a
mind is poured forth, surely it is heard and
accepted of the Divine Being to whom it is
addressed. The morning was thus happily
employed, and in the evening I drank tea
with one of my fellow worshippers, Dr. Wal-
ton who supplied my with much information relative to Elias Hicks and the
general state and prospects of the society
to which he was attached. I found the
Doctor an interesting and an intelligent
man, and though at first sight an ordinary
observer might be excused for supposing him
to be day-labourer, a closer view of him revealed, a high clear forehead and shrewd
and intelligent eye.

The situation of Stroudsberg is very
beautiful, and it may reasonably be

calculated from its many advantage that
at some future day, its increase in population and importance will be considerable.
Monday May 1rst [i.e., 2nd]  Set off in company with
Mr. J. R. a surveyor &c to view some lands
on the Pocono or Broad Mountain, but before
leaving Stroudsburg had the felicity of seeing
an American Militia muster, and though I
had seen Matthew's laughable representation
of one on the stage, the original far surpassed
his copy in all that constitutes a farce. —
There were about 48 men, divided amongst which
number were 4 rifles, one with a broken stock,
2 pistols with laths stuck in the barrell, by
way of elongating them, 2 umbrellas one
of which had no handle, and switches cut from
the woods as they came to rendezvous had
supplied the rest of this formidable assembly
with arms. it was most laughable, and the
parties themselves appeared to be ashamed of
such a farce. —

My companion Mr. J. R. was for an
American a most extraordinary man, and
nothing will hereafter convince me but

40

that <u>one</u> of his parents must have
been an Irish<u>man</u>.  with a red jolly face,
a voice like thunder, spirits so high that neither
themselves or their owner knew how to dispose
of them, with a perfect knowledge of every
place, and a well chosen word for every body,
he was the best guide and instructor that I
could have chosen. We departed and had
the good fortune to be in time for another
training at Hambleton, a village at the
distance of 6 miles. This was a much more
soldier-like affair, and the corps formed a little
regiment which as far as muscular strength
was concerned, would scarcely meet with a
match in Europe. There were crowds of girls
there from the neighbouring country, and as
the evening brought on a scene, which from
its description must very much resemble
an old English wake I regretted not being [able]
to remain long enough to witness it.

　　　We hastened on, and met the ruins
of another company of Militia, and a
proportionate number of girls who were
come to enjoy the scene. —

At about 6 P.M. we began to ascend
the Pocono which here runs nearly 2000
feet, and is covered with an eternal wood.
The Kattanning range, which we had left
at the distance of 16 miles presented at this
sunset hour a most beautiful view. Elevated
far above the surrounding country, and
completely covered with wood, the sun, which
had set to the lower lands, still shed a rosy light upon the long range of mountain
presenting a singular and a glorious spectacle. We reached the Inn and took up
our abode with Mr. Fox, whose estab-
lishment I hereby recommend to all whom
it may concern.

Tuesday May 2 [i.e., 3]. Rose early in the morning and took a guide thro' the woods which
to an European would be quite inexplicable
In one direction they extend through a country
of 2 or 300 miles, and from the rocky nature
of the land are almost impassable for any
but foot passengers. I regretted a thousand
times having brought my horse with me.
I know of nothing more melancholy than

42

and utterly desolate than these primaeval
forests. Were there nothing but green trees
and verdant foliage around, like some of the
groves and woods in the English parks it would
be altogether a different affair: but in these
forests you cannot move a step without meeting
with a fallen and decaying trunk, nor can
your eye look around without beholding every
where the half burnt skeleton of many a once
noble tree. In the woods on the "broad mountain" there are a great number of the purest
springs, which uniting for a creek which
to my certain knowledge contains some
of the finest trout as Mr. J. R. and myself
caught about 60 in the course of an hour.
Our ride back again to the Inn, lay
thro' a part of the forest which had been
burned over last fall, and so long was it
in continuance and so violent in its effects
that it endangered the lives of numerous
settlers: Such a scene of devastation I
never before beheld, every living thing had
abandoned the frightful scene, every appearance of vegetation was destroyed,

the trees yet standing were charred to the
very core, the destructive element had dug
thro' the ground even to their extremest roots
and ploughed up and blackened even the solid
earth. The conflagration had continued to
rage for three weeks and not less than several
hundred thousand acres had been ravaged. —
        These fires which not only destroy the timber
but impoverish the land occur every fall,
and are generally lighted by the hunters who
use this mode of collecting the deer to a
particular spot where they shoot them with
but little trouble, and though a heavy punishment awaits any one <u>detected</u> in setting fire
to the woods, the impossibility of discovery en-
ables them to continue the destructive practice with impunity. The only means which
the settlers in the woods have of preserving
their lives and property is to "fight fire",
by seizing a favourable wind and setting
fire to the adjacent country, thus put a stop
to the coming evil.
        It appears that the spring is not
exempt from these visitations, as on this

44

evening a large fire was visible at
the distance of several miles, as the wind
however was in a favourable direction, no
danger was apprehended.
May 3 [i.e., 4] Wednesday. Returned to Stroudsberg,
saw along the road a Mud turtle and a
water snake. This reminds me that a
son of our last mentioned landlord, had
been bit by a rattle snake, while in the
woods thro' which we had passed. The bite
was given in the month of July, at which
time and in August their venom is supposed to be most fatal. The sufferings that
the boy experienced were for several weeks
most excruciating and his death was hourly
expected. He had been wounded in the heel
but the effects of the poison transferred themselves to his chest and lungs, producing the
most violent pains and vomitings of blood
and bile. The application of tea made from
the bark of white ash, being at last
thought of, its effects were so powerful that
in 15 minutes after taking it, the poison
appeared to be driven to the spot where

the wound was made and he was able
for the first time to sit up, and tho' painful sores formed on his heel and ancle, he
at length entirely recovered. It is said that
the rattle snake is never to be found in the
neighbourhood of this tree, and there appears to
be no doubt of the efficacy of its bark. An
old Hunter even assured me, that if a man
were bitten by a rattle snake, and immediately chewed the bark of the white ash and
swallowed the juice, that no dangerous
consequences would ensue; snakes however
are much less frequently met with in this
part of the country than is generally supposed
to be the case and settlers appear to think
little or nothing about them. —

This part of Pensylvania is inhabited
principally by Germans, and a man who
resides here must positively be acquainted
with the language, or he will be very often
greatly at a loss; the standard of morals
does not appear to stand very high, and
a total absence of refinement pervades the
whole community
Note A. Keller

46

Thursday May 4th [i.e., 5th].      Returned to
Easton by another route called the wind
Gap, the Mountains around which have
an elevation of about 1200 feet. I found
the woods on fire in two places.

I have been told by many here, that
there is a strong prejudice against the English, indulged in by the Americains generally,
and that those feelings have been excited or
at least increased by the unfavourable and
unfair statements of our travellers and review
ers, and many well educated men with
whom I have recently met, express their
disapprobation of the ungenerous behaviour
of Basil Hall, who, while here, was treated
with every attention and kindness, and in return
has given strength to falsehoods and
misapprehensions, which injure the name
and the credit [of] this empire.
Friday May 5 [i.e., 6].   Took my gun and
strolled up the banks of the Delaware
but could get a shot except at Yellow
birds, blue birds and water snipe. crossed
over the river b̶a̶n̶k̶ and returned by the other

side.

Saturday May 6th [i.e., 7th].  Spent part of the day on
a hill which rises at the back of the town
to an elevation of 400 feet. The prospect from
this mount, of the town, the adjacent hills
and ravines clothed with woods, the lush
creek with its mills and waterfalls, and
the broader stream of the Delaware, sometimes streaming between lofty rocks, and at
other times winding thro' the rich valley to the south,
the orchards, the profusion of orchards loaded
with the luxuriant blossom of the peach and
apple, presented a beautiful variety of objects
which detained me there untill sunset;
I fixed my eye upon a lovely spot, where
of all things it would be most delightful
to build a home, and lighten and bless it
with the smiles of —— aye of whom?
Sunday May 7th [i.e., 8th].  A wet and thoroughly miserable day, but being anxious to attend a place
of worship I went into the first I came near
but which, when the service began, unfortunately, proved to be Dutch. Utterly unac-
quainted with the language, I was obliged

to withdraw from outward forms, to inward
service, which I trust was neither unacceptable
or unprofitable. As the evening was rather
finer, I rambled into the country, and avoid-
ing myself of a trifling shower to take shelter under a rustic porch, I entered into
conversation with and old man to whom the
house belonged. I found him interesting &
communicative. He was an old labourer,
who out of his earnings had saved sufficient
to purchase the house and few acres of
land, and had laid by sufficient to support his
wife and child, should he be taken away from
them. The following conversation took place
between us.

I   You live happily thus, I have no doubt then?
L.  I do Sir. I am happy in my work I
am happy at night when I return home, and
all of us sit round the stove together, I smoke
my wife works, and my little girl talks,
and then on Sunday, such a day as this I
seldom go out except to church, for I am
getting rather old, and like to stop at home
when I can.

I. Come Sir, take a cigar with me, and
I hope I am not occupying your time too much.
L. Oh no Sir, I am glad to see you, and so
you are just come from England, times are full
of trouble both there, and all over Europe?
I   They are indeed full of trouble every where, nor
is England much more exempted from trials
than her neighbours. I only hope that the changes
which must take place in the old country,
may be effected quietly, by the mind of the reformer
rather than by the passions of the revolutionists.
L. Your country is very much taxed is it not.
I   Heavily so, and the labourers are but ill paid.
and amongst the agriculturists there were, last year,
strong symptoms of disaffection. I wish that I
could see at home, the same plenty and comforts
and independence that every one enjoys here.
L. I wish you could Sir. This certainly is a happy
country, every man here may do well and live
happy and respectable, and bring up his family
in comfort, and all the children have the best
of education here, and its a land of liberty where
the poor man is equal to the rich, and will
take neither injury or insult from any one.

50.

I  Well Sir I must bid you goodbye, and I
wish you may live long to enjoy the fruits
of your labour; you are another convincing
proof, that the idle man is not the most
happy, and that a life of honest employment
as it is the most truly honourable, is also
in reality the most happy.
L.  Goodbye Sir, and call in again any time.
I shall be glad to see you.

Such was a part of our
conversation, and so true it is that America is
a land of plenty and of comfort; none are in
want, for the healthy there is always employment
and liberal pay, for the infirm there is always
a charitable asylum; A more convincing
proof that this is true, can hardly be advanced
than this fact, that in a tour of a great part
of Pensylvania, I have not met with one individual, who either wants or solicited charity.
what a melancholy j̸o̸u̸r̸n̸e̸y̸ contrast would a
journey over the same number of miles in the
Br. Dominions present. Oh my country my
noble but unfortunate country, what have
those rulers to answer for, whose wretched

policy has plunged thee into such difficulty
and distress.
Monday May 8th [i.e., 9th]. Went to a review of a
battalion at the distance of 6 miles from Easton.
The troops were of a much better order than I
had expected to see, and presented altogether a very
soldier like and formidable appearance. One
circumstance which took place, may serve
to illustrate the character of her soldiers and
the nature of their discipline. The captain of
a very fine volunteer corps, upon being placed
by the brigade general on the left, instead of
the right, very coolly marched his men out of
the field, and passing close by the general and his
staff, performed the customary evolutions, in a
nother field hard by. The number of spectators
men women and children must have been
at least 3000, and such a pell mell assembly
I never before had the honour of meeting
with — men women children horses dogs
pigs, fiddling firing swearing dansing drinking
but all went off, guns and pistols into the bargain
with a most praiseworthy degree of good humour
and harmlessness.

52

Tuesday May 10th. Fell into company in
the morning with an intelligent man, who
was intimately acquainted with many of the
most influential men in the state. His opinion
of the President Jackson was very high, both
as to talent and principle, and as he had been
employed in negotiations with the Indians
at three different times, I found his company
very acceptable and entertaining. I discovered
afterwards that he had been a catholic Priest.
You will find Sir, said he, a great difference
between the common Europeans and the common
Americains, it is not so much in the higher
classes that a want of similarity prevails. No
there is here an aristocracy, much resembling
that of England, for the absence of titles is but
of trifling consequence, the thing exists and
will I suppose as long as the principles of
human nature remain the same, but you
will find in the lower orders of Americains a
degree of shrewdness, the existence of which
under so rough an exterior, you would hardly
expect, and there is more than all, a sense
of natural dignity, not pride, of individual

worth, not conceit, which characterizes
him from all other men. He knows that his
country is essentially free, that he himself has
a voice in the affairs of its government, he
as both seen and read enough to judge of the
effects of priestcraft and kingcraft and lordcraft
in other countries and worlds would not tempt
him to sacrifice one job or one tittle of individual or national independence. —

In the afternoon, I strolled up the banks
of the Delaware, my favourite route, in company with a good natured and merry little Frenchman, and discovering that a large lumber
raft had grounded, we went to the assistance
of the man. After some very hard work we
got it off the shoal, and returned home upon
it. it was composed of 70 immense trunks of
Hemlock, and had been brought about 75 miles
down the river. We at first moved very
slowly as the stream was deep, but when we
came to an island which divided the river into
two equal parts, the rapids hurled us along at
the rate of 10 miles an hour, and a most delightful voyage we had.

54.

Wednesday May 11th. Set off in the
stage for Philadelphia, at 5 AM. the
morning beautiful, and the weather which
had been for a long time exceedingly cold for
the season, appeared to be now settled into the
delightful temperature of the month of May;
the first part of the journey, as long indeed
as we continue in the vicinity of the Delaware
the country is picturesque and beautiful, after
we leave the river however, through a great
part of Bucks county, the land becomes poor
and barren, and the romantic character of
the country disappears. Their roads are really
inexcusably bad, the jolting is most uncivil
and often leads to adventures ludicrous enough.
For instance, an old man of rather more
than 300 weight was precipitated into the lap of
a little cross old lady, who shortly after left
the stage in the full conviction that one half
her bones were broken, and I very nearly
knocked out one of my own eyes, while attempting
to put my hands into my breeches pockets.
One great recommendation to Americain
travelling is this, there are no coachmen

and guards to pay, a circumstance
which to a man who has travelled through
England, is enough to redeem the character
of the whole empire. From Easton to P.
is 56 miles which occupied 10 hours. I was
too much fatigued to examine any part
of the city that night, although my anxiety
to see it, had been continually whetted by the
intimation that it was the most beautiful
city in the world. —
Thursday May 12. Called upon Mr. J. T.
whom I found an agreable sensible gentleman, and one very ready to render a kindness to any one. In his conversation, he
spoke highly of America, though he could
not [help] smiling at some of its characteristics
and respecting emigration, he thinks that
many people are disappointed, though any
one possess[e]d of the knowledge of a trade, or
tact enough to make himself generally useful
must meet with encouragement. But above
all says he, America is the country for a
man who has sufficient to keep him in
independence. The state of things is such

56

that he can purchase a greater
quantity of comfort and happiness here
than in any other country in the world.
Nor is there that absence of luxury and
refinement, which *in* Europeans generally
imagine to exist, and it is not so completely a land of independence and equality
that riches cannot command a great degree
of consideration and attention.

The weather has become too warm
to take much exercise, and it is pleasanter
at home than out of doors.

<u>Friday May 13th</u>. Had some leisure
to look over the city, which is certainly
a very delightful place. It is, with the
exception of one or two streets near the
river, laid out in right angles and many
of the streets present strait and parallel
rows of good houses 2 miles at least,
in length, while many and beautiful
trees, in front of the houses in even their
busiest thoroughfares, cheer the eye with
their verdant foliage.

There does not appear to be anything

like an equal quantity of shipping in
this port to that of New York. There are
but few large ships come up the river,
the number of Coasters is however very
considerable and rapidly increasing, and
the internal trade of the city, as well
as its connexion with the Western States
is sufficient to keep all the citizens well
employed.

Saturday May 14. Wrote to Mr. Vaughan, and to Fish Grennell &Co. Met
with a fine intelligent boy of 12 years old
who spoke like a man of 30 in some
conversation which I had with him on
the subject of slavery. It is certainly a
fact, that in this country the mind is
developed at an early age, and education is now so much spread and perfec-
ted that the rising generation bid fair
to be a new people. There are not here
the profound and perfect in art in science
and in classic lore, so much perhaps as
in an old country, but there is a general
circulation, a constant interchange and use

of practical knowledge, and information available for the great purposes of
existence, which is of much greater importance: the journals are almost num-
berless and generally well conducted, but
if we may judge from their occasional
extracts and critiques there is a mani
fest respect for the literature of England
still cherished amongst them.

Attended the Theatre where there
was some tolerable performance, but
not a very large or very genteel audience.
The Chestnut St. theatre is rather less
than the Haymarket in London.
Sunday May 15th. Went to the Unitarian church "like a good boy" as "Aunty
says", in company with Mr. Taylor
who after the service introduced me to
Mr. Furniss from whom I had heard
a very eloquent and manly discourse.

The congregation was large and respec
table, and a degree and kind of religious
feeling appeared to pervade the assembly,
which was truly gratifying

The morning service here begins at 10
the evening at 8 oclock: a late hour indeed
but the pleasantest by far, in a climate
so warm as this.      I was surprized
to find that nightfall is the favourite
hour for promenade amongst the higher
orders here, but it is by far the most
delightful, as after sunset, a fine fresh
breeze almost invariably springs up,
"Spreading o'er all after the parching heat
Its pleasant coolness."

     These two lines being a quotation
from my own works, I am reminded
how completely I have abandoned poetical
composition, or rather how completely it
has abandoned me. I have found that
for some years the "fire of poesy" has been
gradually abating, and I must now settle
down in the sad conviction that it is
fairly gone out.

     The Americains are decididly a church
going people, for the places of worship numerous
as  they are, are crowded to suffocation.
There is of course in a country like this

60

an almost infinite variety of Xtianity
and to an European it is truly delightful
to perceive how unity of action in all that
concerns the wellbeing of a nation, is capa-
ble of being preserved amid the differences which
exist in religious opinions. To one also who
has been accustomed to the costly church estab-
lishment of England and the legal robbery for
the support of its tithe-owners, to one who
has heard continually their haughty and im
pertinent assumption of superiority, a noble
lesson may be learned from observing how
little religion needs the arm of the law to protect
it. The churches are filled, the ministers are
respected, and what is no doubt equally impor
tant, are well paid, yet their power and
their influence is founded only upon, and
perpetuated by the real importance of religion
to the human soul. There is no doubt in
my mind that the divine religion of Jesus has
been both misunderstood and misused, that
it has been obscured and corrupted, but still
it contains so much that is really good, and
which no circumstances or representations

can separate wholly from it, that it may
be safely left, as far as regards its spread
and influence to the hearts and consciences
of men, without being supposed for a moment to be dependent upon legal authority
for support.  I have said that religion
is widely spread amongst this people, a
few remarks upon its influence on society
may not be out of place. The religious
world here as els[e]where is much afflicted with
the disease called "cant", and bigotry and phari-
saic ideas of righteousness peculiar grace and
particular election are promulgated zealously
and most devoutly believed, the ladies Heaven bless them, always the first to be influenced
where sensibility is concerned, nor less back-
ward in active exertion where a work of real
or imagined kindness is to be done, are peculiarly under the influence of religious enthu-
siasm, and adding their powerful means of
persuasion to the thunders of the minister, a
huge and heterogeneous mass of ~~societies~~ religious
societies in all their ramifications of schools
clan meetings, bible tract and missionary

associations overrun the face of the earth.
This spirit which has undoubtedly been developed so much, and the energies of which have
not been kept either within the bounds of
good policy or true religion, has created a
re-action in the minds of many upright
and probably some, more worldly minded men,
who view with jealousy and treat with no
small degree of scorn and harshness, the grow-
ing influence, which by such means as these
the priests are gaining over the minds of the
people, and dread not a little that at some
future day that influence will be extended
to the constitution, an evil which all true
friends of mankind and their country will
pray and strive that God in his goodness may
avert. —
Monday May 16th. Called upon Mr. J. Vaughan
in company with Mr. J. T. and found him
a very old, and a very interesting man; an
active and efficient member of the general
society of mankind, a warm and sincere friend
of his country, his kindest and most fervent
feelings appear to be concentrated in the

welfare of the religious society of which
he is a member. His sitting room is
hung around with portraits of its most dis
tinguished advocates, and his memory is
stored with a fund anecdotes relative to
them and many Xtian worthies of the old
school.        It is a noble and a happy sight
to see an old and a good man, one who is
full of years and honour, look back with
feelings of affection and pride, to the religious
connexions and friendships of years that are
long gone by, and recognize in the valued
portraits of those whose place on earth know-
eth them no more, the resemblance of those
who have worshipped at the same altar, and
endured the same trials for conscience sake,
it is a sight yet more beautiful to behold
him looking forward to a future state, as
to a happier land where he shall be again
united, in the same labours and the same
affections, to those whom he has known
and loved below. — This day I sent a letter
to Canada to my brother Phil

64 Tuesday May 17th

Occupied the morning in examining
the contents of the Museum which though
not very large, contains a considerable variety
of curiosities. amongst them may be numbered
relics of Indian warfare, birds beasts fishes
minerals fossils, and in particular the very
nearly perfect skeleton of a mammoth..
The size of this enormous beast bears about
the same proportion to an elephant as an
elephant to a calf and I believe that a
simile of this kind will give you a more correct
idea of its magnitude than a detail of its
actual measurement, at any rate it is
a great deal less trouble.

In the afternoon I called upon
Mr. J. Cadbury, whom I found an intelligent and pleasing man, a quaker, mana-
ger of a wholesale concern in the city. I
went with him to the store, and was surprized to find that in very many cotton goods,
particularly of the heavy kind, the Americain
manufacturers can produce goods at a rather
lower rate than those of England.

Wednesday May 18th [65]

     Was called up at 6 oclock A.M. and informed that a gentleman was waiting to see me. Upon going down I found Mr. Vaughan waiting to take me to breakfast with him, as I should there meet with a grandson of Dr. Priestly's, a man about the age of 35 and sensible and agreable. — Every one rises early here, and the distribution of meals is about as follows. breakfast 7 to 8, dinner 1 to 2, supper 7 to 8. These are all their repasts, and at dinner they eat with a rapidity that electrified me, nor do they indulge by sitting after it to take their wine. Almost every man smokes here, and cigars are not quite as expensive a luxury as in <u>dear</u> England.    Sent a letter this afternoon to Greg directed to Nachetochez Louisiana, a sort of forlorn hope, and sent rather from a sense of duty than in the anticipation of receiving an answer.

Thursday May 19th  Employed the day in reading at the Atheneum, and called in the afternoon, in company with Mr. T.

upon Rev Mr. Furniss, whom I found to
be a very sensible and a very pleasing man
with that cheerfulness of mind and suavity
of manners which I have frequently noticed
to belong to the ministers of this sect. Supped
with Mr. Taylor and passed a pleasant evening. In returning home, my attention
was caught by a confused and mingled
sound, proceeding from a long low building
in Fifth St., I believe. This interesting edifice
was one story high and divided into different
compartments, and a nearer approach revealed
to me that it was devoted to religious purposes, and the fearful sounds proceeded from
some devotees, who were engaged in their exer-
cises in this religious gymnasium; I hope
that my mind is not disposed to ridicule
anything, which connected with religion and
morality, has a just claim upon my respect
but, it is impossible I think, to avoid looking
with pity or disgust, upon the gross perversion
displayed by some of these people, of the simple
and practical nature of the religion of Jesus.

The same spirit I have seen displayed

in several other churches in this place
and the following sentiments utter[e]d by a popu-
lar preacher to a large congregation does
not confer much credit upon either the prea
cher or the people, for either candour or charity
"Stick my Friends" said the preacher in his
elegant phraseology, stick to old fashioned
Methodism once, stick to it twice I say,
(and then in a voice of thunder), stick to it
3 times I say right or wrong.
Friday May 20
No. 2 Wrote to Mrs. Harwood, detailing
my examination of her lands, and advising
a sale to be made in England &c &c, and the
same evening wrote to I[.] Rogers and Clooper
all their answers to be addressed to the Post
Office Philadelphia. —
Saturday May 21rst
          Passed the day principally at the
Atheneum in reading &c. —
Sunday May 22
          Attended divine Service twice at the
Unitarian Chapel. The weather is now
becoming very warm, but there is a

fine fresh breeze which renders the heat
somewhat more supportable. This reminds
me of an anecdote of the late Dr. Priestly
who upon his arrival in this country, was
saying to a friend, I do not know it is but,
although the rise of the mercury indicates
a warmer temperature than in the old country, I feel the heat much less. Oh Doctor
replied his friend, no wonder the room is not
so close, look how much higher the ceiling
is, pointing to the sky, which in this climate is clear and lofty and blue.

<u>Monday May 23</u>. Spent the greater part of
the day at the Atheneum, but occupied the
afternoon in writing to Mr. Hack, respecting
the transmission of b̸i̸l̸l̸s̸ letters of credit for
me.

<u>Tuesday May 24th.</u> Attended the theatre in
the evening, the play performed was The
Stranger, but altogether wretchedly <u>done</u>.

<u>Wednesday May 25</u>. Looking anxiously
for English news and letters, as I wished
to set out upon my northern tour. —
I hear so much of Niagara, the

visit to its falls is so much talked of
even here, that I must contrive to
perform the northern, shame would it be
to return to England without having beheld
this greatest of all natural curiosities.
W̶e̶d̶n̶e̶s̶d̶a̶y̶ Thursday May 26. Attended at the
general assembly of the Presbyterian churches
partly to perceive the usual mode of their conduc
ting business, but chiefly to witness the trial of
a Mr. Barnes, who it appears has been guilty
of the heinous crime of something approaching to
Heterodoxy — shocking! what will the world come
to? The moderator whose situation was by no
means enviable, and who seemed to be an a-
miable and a clever man, had no small diffi
culty in keeping the members in order, and considerable warmth of discussion took place;
The room became so exceedingly crowded and hot
that I was glad the stormy atmosphere.

The were a great many ladies present,
and it is a fact highly creditable to the strength
of their nerves, that no fainting, a l'Anglaise
took place amongst them.

The presbyterians form a large & an

70

influential body. They are regarded however by the great body of the people, with no
small degree of jealousy, being suspected of
designs to connect the state with their system
of religion. Thanks however to the lessons afforded
by the history of past, and the experience of
present ages, the Americains have become
rather too shrewd to yield up their liberty to
any set of men, whether priests or politicians
In the afternoon I strolled several miles down
the banks of the Delaware, which is here a
large and important river, the bassin
of which is adorned with a large number
of vessells, principally steam boats, and
schooners or brigs used in the coasting trade
which is here very large. There are a
considerable number of snipe along the
banks of this river, and no small quantity
of water snakes. In passing along a bank
with my attention fixed upon a number of
large sturgeon which had been left ashore
I trod upon and killed 2 snakes which
were lying across the path, and with whose
murder I should certainly have dispensed

The country in this neighbourhood is low and very swampy, and cannot I apprehend be very healthy. Friday May 27. Encouraged by the fineness of the morning I determined to take a little excursion into the country, and putting on my shooting dress, and taking my gun, I walked out to the water works at Fair Mount which are indeed well worth the trouble of a visit They are situated on the River Schulkyll, at a distance of 2 miles from the city. The machinery is worked by water power, and the water is elevated to the height of about 100 feet, an elevation sufficient to supply a powerful rush of the precious element to all parts of the city. The works are open free of expense for public view, and the scenery of the place is as beautiful as the object is praiseworthy. I took a boat and rowed a few miles up the River the shores of which abound in the picturesque It is a favourite amusement with the Philadelphians to come here and promenade or fish, they may occasionally find a shot or two at Wild Duck or Snipe.

<u>Saturday May 28.</u>

The day unfavourable — at home writing & reading. Since the introduction of
the Schulkyll water, there has been no return
of the dangerous fevers to which the city was
formerly subject.

<u>Sunday May 29th.</u>

Attended Divine Worship as
usual, and was much pleased with the dis-
courses delivered by the Red. Mr. Gannett who
is a colleague of Dr. Channing. The heat this
day was intense the thermometer at 6 oclock
P.M. being 84. Observed at church in the
evening 2 customs differing from those in
England — the gentlemen using fans, (nay
even the doorkeeper was sitting down thus
laudably employed,) & several gentlemen of
respectability attending in such dresses as
white tan [?] jacket

May 30th Monday — At the Atheneum
the weather intensely hot, the thermometer
standing at 94 in the shade. Attended at
the theatre, in order to see and to form
an estimate of the greatest actor

amongst the Americains Mr. Hackett.
His acting is good but certainly inferior
to that of the English. I could not but
notice the dearth of beauty and gentility in
the audience which was however pretty numerous. A trait of nationality excited my
interest. In the course of the drama the name
of Washington was introduced as the Father
and the Saviour of his country: the ~~burst~~
~~of~~ applause at this sentence was electrifying
it was not ~~merely~~ the unsubstantial accla-
mation of a party, but one burst of feeling.
The memory of that man appears to be re-
vered and enshrined in the hearts of his country-
men. There cannot perhaps be a more for-
cible proof of the happiness of this empire
and the value of its institutions, than the
fact, the emigrants no matter from
what country, soon identify themselves with
the natives, and feel and act with an e-
qually deep interest in the welfare of the
States.
Tuesday May 31st. Weather exceeding
ly sultry. Visited Mr. Furniss in

the afternoon and had a long and interesting conversation with him. He appears to
think that the demand for Unitarian preachers
in the west is immense, and I was surprized to
find that there are 15000 Congregns. of a sect called
Christians, the principles of which are decidedly
Unitarian.

<u>Wednesday June 1rst</u>.  Impossible to take
any exercise so I remained at home in
reading &c, and in writing a discourse, but
in the evening I went to Swain's bath
and spent half an hour in the water.

  The news from Europe excite here the war-
mest interest. The struggle of the Poles with
their scoundrel like oppressor is regarded with
the greatest anxiety, and the political state
of G. Britain has fixed the eyes of this people
upon her. God grant that the struggle may
end only in the triumph of liberty and justice
Thursday June 2nd

  Employed the morning in writing
a sermon or at least part of one. . . Is it
not likely that I might employ myself
usefully and advantageously in this

country, in the ministerial profession
Mr F. has kindly encouraged the idea, and
says that he will ensure my success. I
must however wait advices from England
before I can finally decide. My course of
life for the last 3 mo. has convinced me that
idleness is not happiness, and I know of nothing
which could effectually administer to the
comfort of my life, than a devotion of all my
best energies to the fulfillment of the interesting
duties of that office.

<u>Friday June 3</u>. The weather a little cooler
and I determined to make a little excursion
into the country, and accordingly went several
miles up the Schulkyll. I found the scenery
exquisitely beautiful, and a romantic tavern
at which I found an English family and where
I passed several hours. At my return in the
evening the atmosphere was absolutely illumi-
ned with fire-flies — the vivid and wandering
light of which form a beautiful object, and
to a northern European. —

Saturday June 4th. Exceedingly hot and at home
all day reading &c.

[76] <u>Sunday June 5th</u>. Attended Divine Service
at the Unitarian Church and spent the day
happily.
Monday June 6th. Employed the morning
in looking over old letters & papers. They inspird.
me (consistently with all the laws of romance)
with a deep feeling of melancholy. In
particular a review of the letters connected
with Jeanette my old flame, inflicted upon
me a most grievous heartache — "mais
tout cela est passé["].
Tuesday June 7. Writing in the morning — visited the Franklin Institute in
the afternoon — the room supplied with
more newspapers than books, and containing some interesting models of machinery.
Wednesday June 8th. The day employed
in that hardest of all work, viz, doing
nothing — Theatre in the evening.
Thursday — Visited Wests celebrated picture of "Christ rejected". a noble specimen
of art, and there is so much of
character and effect in the picture

that it is scarcely possible to return
from a contemplation of it, without being
a wiser and a better man. spent the evening with Joel Cadbury and wife, very
good people and gave me some delicious
strawberries and cream. children rather
squally that's all. heat very oppressive
Friday June 10th. Wearied of Philadel
phia, so took the stage to Manayunk
and returned by the river Schuylkill, a
description of the banks of which I have
before given.
Saturday June 11th. — Horridly rainy day
and fatigued with my yesterday expedition
in all day reading.
<u>Sunday</u> — Attended divine service as usual
spent a pleasant evening with the Taylors
Monday June 13. visited Wests exquisite
painting of t̶h̶e̶ "Christ rejected" — again for
it is one which will bear a repeated visit
in the evening attended a concert given by
the band of the city guards of Boston. The
music was exceedingly good and the audience
numerous and genteel. There were 1400 present.

78  Tuesday June 14.

Rain. rain. rain.

Wednesday June 15 — Visited the Pensylvania Hospital, a noble institution founded
by Penn, it is rich, and productive of
great good, as it generally accommodates
250 patients.

Thursday June 16th.  Rainy. The thunder
tremendous, and the lightning struck 2
places in the city.

Friday June 17th.  Employed principally
in making commercial enquiries — made
up my mind to set off for Canada.

Saturday June 18 — two months since I
landed — query how much have I learned
since I have been here? don't know — how
much have I spent? 150 Dollars and far
from being either industrious or extrava-
gant, called on Mr. Furniss who gives
me letters of recommendation to various
parts —

Sunday June 19.  Attended Mr. F
as usual and heard very eloquent ser
mon. wrote to Courtauld &Co,

acknowledging the receipt of their
goods on Monday June 12th. [13th?] giving inf
ormation of the sale of drapes in this country, pointing out obstacles in the way of
the sale of these and recommending no more
consignments.
Monday June 20. Left Pa. at 6. AM
in the Swan steam boat, voyaged abt.
35 miles up the Delaware, the scenery of
which is anything but interesting, in this
part of the river. The stream itself is
very wide, but the shore on both side[s]
is low and tame. There are great quan
tities of Sturgeon in this stream, and
almost every moment you are startled
with the sudden appearance of one of
those frightful fish, jumping to the height
of 4 or 5 feet above the water, and then
splashing in again. Steamboat very
full — breakfast bad and dear, my
companions hum drum, but to my great
relief found out an Atheist, with whom
I maintained an argument of 10 or 15 miles
in length — felt very thankful

80.

Landed from the boat at Trenton
a miserable imitation of a town, the
soil dry and barren, altogether flat,
stale and unprofitable. Passed through
Princetown a much prettier place, and
the seat of a college and theological
seminary both handsome buildings.
Arrived at New Brunswick, and set
sail, or rather paddled to New York.
Upon landing there, after ordering my
luggage to the American Hotel, went in
quest of Mr. Vaughan, Brooman &c. and
found them at their old lodgings. I was
much struck and hurt too, (men. usually,
the case) by the appearance of both of
them particularly the latter, for since
my departure, having lost the benefit of
my precept and example, they had indulged in too exclusive and absorbing an att
achment to brandy; lectured them upon
the subject with great pathos and energy
upon the occasion — so much affected that,
I was obliged to treat them with a little of
it, in order to keep up their spirits.

Wednesday June 21rst.
Myself this day in a very bad temper
for I was put into a damp bed at the
Hotel, and a rheumatic pain settled in
my knee so that I can scarcely walk.
very lame — look awkward, but never mind
will look as amiable and walk as slow
as I can, and no doubt I shall be considered
an "interesting invalid". Went to a glass
to see how I looked — death and the devil
my cheeks are as rosy, and my frame as
jolly as an English Foxhunter, very provoking to look so well.
Wednesday June 22. Started at seven in
the morning for Albany in a fine steam
boat of the same name; The route lies
up the river Hudson, a wide deep and
romantic stream. The scenery along its
banks a distance of 150 miles from N.Y.
to Albany is of a varied character. The
wild and the mild, the rough and the
smooth ~~succeeding~~ following each other in rapid succession. On the western bank, a singular
range of rocks continues for 20 miles, and
varying in height from 100 to 500 feet

82

and about 60 miles from New York
there are some mountains on either side
which rise to an elevation of 1500 feet.
The views here are very romantic, and there
are many spots rendered interesting by the
transactions which took place during
the war between Engd. and this country —
Mem. I can here copy largely from the
Northern Traveller, it will pass for original, not that I need anything of that
kind, but such as unprecedented thing
as an <u>original work</u>, would never meet
with encouragement. — The river varies
in this distance from 1/2 mile to 3 miles
wide, and except near to Albany is very
deep. In the vicinity of Albany the river contracts very much in width and becomes
much more shallow, as it was with some
difficulty that the steamboat could pass over
some of the shallows. We arrived there at
about 9 Oclock having been 14 hours in the
water. The voyage has however been performed in 10 1/2 hours by the North America
steamboat.

Thursday June 23rd

Having been unfortunately put into a damp bed at New York, which atrocious carelessness of the innkeeper had entailed upon me his innocent victim a severe rheumatic aff[l]iction, I found it requisite to remain at Albany during one day, and although it was exceedingly damp, I found means to amuse myself in viewing the public buildings of the town. The number of inhabitants may perhaps amount to about 24000 or rather more, there is an appearance of considerable business in the town, as it [is] here that the great Erie Canal joins the Hudson, affording means for the interchange of agricultural and commercial produce between N.Y. and a vast extent of western country. Albany is also the seat of the government of the state of N.Y. and from this circumstance derives of course a considerable degree of consequence — I forgot to name the beautiful object of scenery presented by the Catskill mountains in the voyage up the Hudson. The bold summits of these hills are about 4000 feet above the level of the sea.

Friday June 24th. Found myself at
4 o'clock A.M. in the middle of the canal, and
a fog so dense, that if it had been good you
could have fairly eaten it, on board one of
the Packet boats which travel from Albany to
Buffalo, as the sun ascended however the day
became very pleasant and being joined by two
respectable and intelligent men, the time passed
very pleasantly. At 10 A.M. we reached Schenec-
tady, a busy and very thriving village. During
the remainder of the day our attention was
continually called to the beautiful river of the
Mohawk, which runs very near to the canal
for 150 miles, and over which the canal is
carried by aqueduct of 7 or 800 feet in length
in two places.
Saturday June 25th. Enjoyed another delightful
day, and passed a most romantic spot, called
Little Falls, where the Mohawk descends perhaps 30 feet or more through channels worn
in the solid rock. The canal passes beneath
some very high and beautiful hills and at last
conducts the voyager to Utica, at which busy
and beautiful town I slept that night.

Sunday June 26th. —

Utica is a town rapidly increasing
and one which, more perhaps than any other
excepting Rochester has been advanced in
importance by the canal. But this is Sunday
so we must talk about something else. —
At 7 A.M. I set off on Horseback for Trenton
as I was anxious to see the Falls and had
also a letter of introduction to a family at
that place. — Upon arriving at Mr. Mappe
I was received with the greatest degree of kindness and hospitality, and I was fortunate
enough to have it in my power in some
measure to return their civilities by performing
Divine Service for the congregation to which
they belonged, and whose minister was una-
voidably absent.

Monday June 27th. — Still at Mr. M. where
every thing is done to make a stranger com-
fortable, they are altogether indeed a happy
and a fine family, and one in the bosom of
which Christian love and christian happiness
have made their home — The day lowering
and rainy and myself desperately lame.

86.

Tuesday June 28th. The day
still uncomfortable, but persuaded by a
few glimmerings of sunshine to visit the falls
accompanied by Mr. M. eldest son. — They
are at a distance of about 3 miles from the
village, and at the entrance of a wood which
lies on the left side, is a pleasant house
of refreshment for those who visit the scenery, and where horses or carriages must be left,
as there is no passing through the forest with
them. — The bank which is about 100 feet
high and nearly perpendicular is descended
by a flight of steps, at the bottom of which
you find yourself on a broad large of rock and
directly before the torrent rushes furiously
by in a narrow channel. Looking up
the ravine from this spot the feelings are
powerfully affected; huge precipices of solid
rock rise on either side, while the unim-
aginable luxuriance of foliage on their sumit
and in the intervals between them, and while
it adds to the richness and beauty, takes
away from the aspect of wildness and
desolation which would otherwise be the

master characteristic of the scene.
Here you arrive at a view of the first
fall 33 feet in height, to which you advance
by a path blasted from the solid rock, the
passage of which, though not very dangerous
is sufficiently so to render the visit more
exciting. It is when in a parrallel line with
the rock over which the water is precipitated,
that the view of this fall is the most imposing
as a part of its broad sheet is obscured by an
intervening rock from the eye of the visitor
when he first enters the ravine. You continue
your course from this spot, partly under a
low projection of rock, untill you find yourself on a broad level of the same adamantine
substance, and it is here, that overpowering
magnificence of the great fall meets the won-
dering eye. A huge mass of rock fills up
the avenue to the height of 100 feet, the water
precipitating itself first 40 feet, then descending in a tremendous rapid 15 or 20 feet more
and finally projecting its liquid silver over
another precipice into a deep basin 40
feet below. At the highest elevation of

88

these rocks you ascend a few feet to
a rural retreat, where you can be refreshed
by repose and repast (Only think of this
unsentimental people calling the place a
grocery) where you can enter your name
in a book for the satisfaction of the next curious
visitor, and on the pages of which you may,
inscribe any sentiment or poetical rhapsody,
you like; a privilege inestimable to the
infinity of small poets who visit the place
one of these, a young lady, has left the following powerful testimony to the high degree of
task and genius produced by the "great march".
  I'll tell my mother when I go home
  I've seen the water & all its foam
Notwithstanding the lively emotion and ex
quisite sensibility which must have dictated
these touching lines, the author had so much
strength of mind as to enable her to write so
steadily, that I am credibly informed, the document is (by a reference to the first principles
of pothooks and straight strokes) actually legible.
  Beyond this place and from it is
visible another fall 14 feet high. Above

this we arrive at a broad platform of
rock, over which hangs a huge precipice at
the highest elevation stands a lofty cedar
the appearance of which is very singular,
and from its summit, until last year, a
small stream, which in the fall became converted into a shower bath, but visitors are
now unfortunately deprived of this luxury.
On the day of my visit, as there was a
substitute in the shape of a drenching shower
of rain, I did not pause to mourn over the
absence of the original. Still further above
is another wild and broken cascade, and here
I thought of returning. We retraced our
steps to the grocery — faugh-hermitage let
us call it, and having there secured some
of the beautiful crystals which are found in
abundance amongst the rocks, we retired to
the inn through the woods, a path which
I would recommend to all visitors as from
the edge of the precipices, the scenery of the
rocks and water, viewed from such as elevation assumed a different but a not less
glorious aspect. —

At our return, the family of which
I was an inmate carried me to a tea
party at the house of Mr. Perkins, a
very intelligent and superior man, with
a charming family — one daughter in
particular. Oh — ah — Humph. —
Wednesday June 29th. Returned to Utica
and during the ride, enjoyed a delightful
opportunity for the exercise of the Christian
virtue patience, as we were about 4 hours
coming 13 miles. —

There appear to have been immense
numbers of Swiss pass through this town
on their road to the west, and during
last year and this it is supposed that
their numbers would amount to several
thousand. They appear poor and dirty, —
the former qualification is disputed by many,
but the latter accomplishment I have never
yet heard questioned. —
Thursday June 30th. — Reading and writing
a sermon for the 3rd of July — walked out in
the evening to enjoy the sun and saw a y[oun]g
man sitting on a rail, looking at

the summit, with paper and pencil before him
his mouth and eyes wide open, drinking in large
draughts of inspiration — Mem. ought to be a
temperance society to guard over such dangerous tendency to drink so inordinately of the
waters of Helicon. — Met with an Englishman
whom I had previously seen at Easton — In
his journey to America he appeared to [have] strength-
ened and confirmed the prejudices with which
he came to U.S.

Friday July 1. Returned to my kind Hosts
at Trenton, and gladly exchanged the desolation of a Hotel, where you care for no one
and no one cares for you, for the comfort &
the Hospitality of a private family. —

Saturday July 2. Again visited Trenton
Falls in company with Mr. M. Miss. M. M.
Miss Salter, with C & J.M. a pleasant party
and a favourable day — the waters of the
creek had been considerably augmented by the
late rains, and the falls presented in consequence
a much sublimer spectacle — We also went
up higher than I had done the former day
and encountered not a few perils.

92

Toil and peril were however amply
repaid by the exceeding beauty of the scene, &
I left it with a sigh of regret that I should
in all prob.y. visit it no more.
Sunday July 3. Was employed a great part
of the day in preaching. The morning discourse
being upon the sub.t of civil and religious lib.y
        Was taken very ill with a bilious attack
in the evening
Monday July 4. — Aroused early by the firing
of cannon, it being considered almost a religious
duty to explode gunpowder in its various
manifestations of cannon squib cracker &c
but very ill all day, and obliged to have
recourse to medical advice —
Tuesday July 5 — Still unwell and confined
to the house
Wednesday July 6 — prepared to leave in the
afternoon but the coach full — mem I was
really very glad of it, for I quite love this
family and dread to be separated from them.
Thursday July 7. Actually set off, after
giving & receiving affectionate adieus to & fro.
my kind friends.

remained at Utica a few hours and
then took the canal boat, that is the canal
boat took me on my journey. These boats
are very convenient and very inconvenient
the first because you travel without fatigue
the second, because men women and squall[in]g
children fill up the whole space around you.
"There is no peace", and although the canal
is stagnant enough, yet on its "still waters"
there is none of the tranquillity of which they
are said to be the emblem.
Friday July 8. — Still on the canal, our journey becomes more interesting we are in sight
of a sweet little lake abt. 10 miles in length
and 5 in breadth, and on the far side is a
thriving town called Liverpool — not so large
as its prototype, but yet a handsome town.
In this neighbourhood are the great salt works
which now supply almost the whole of US.
The drying vats cover many acres of ground — it
is sold at 10/ –. 1 1/4 dollar per barrell. — After
spending another night on the canal, and
having passed through many thriving villages I
landed at Pittsford an

94

Saturday July 9th. —
After an uncomfle. breakfast at the
Inn, set off for the residence of Mr.
Billingshurst — a brother in law of Mr. J Brown
of Ditchling. I found them out and
was welcomed like an old friend. They
lived in a good brick house, the old log
one having been removed. — Returned
in the afternoon to fetch my luggage
as I intended to spend several days ar
Mr. B. The weather chill & I ill.
Sunday July 10th Preached two
sermons to very att. congregns. — There
are in this neighbourhd. many Universts.
or call them Unitarians if you will
much fatigued in the evening. —
Monday July 11. Exceedingly unwell
quite knocked up and the rheumatizm
returnd. to my knee. — Mr. B. is an old
preacher — a venerable old man 72 years
old. mighty in the scriptures — a "leetle"
prosy withall. His wife about the same
age — having a numerous family of
children grand and great grand &c —

Tuesday July 12th.
Still very unwell but induced to visit
the village 2 1/2 miles distant to deliver an
evening lecture. had a large and an
attentive congn. and great anxiety expressd.
that my services should be repeated.

In the morning of this day visited
several individuals, and found them all
liberally inclined
Wednesday July 13th. Left Pittsford for
Rochester, a busy town of the great
Erie Canal — a popn. of 11,000 — and 16
years since there was not one house on
the site of this now flourishg. town. —

There is an abundance of water
power here, the Genessee, a considerable
river, having a considerable fall. —
on the NE of the town, one of these
cataracts assumes an appearance of the
sublime. The whole body of this river
falls 96 feet in one unbroken sheet, over
a ledge of rocks stretching across the river. A
waterfall however looks sadly out of place
in the midst of a populous town.

96

Thursday July 14th.

Left Rochester for Buffalo. The road
exceedingly bad. This part of the state of
NY is covered with wood, and though here
and there you meet with a good farm,
yet the ground is generally so low and
swampy, as to appear unfit for cultivation.
There are however very few instances of
ague & fever in this district. Buffalo
is a thriving town on the Banks of Lake
Erie, where the St Lawrence receives its surplus
waters; the waters of the lake are very clear
and looked so much like the ocean that
the scene reminded me of auld lang syne. —
In the last war, one house only was left
standing by the Br. army, who sacked the
place, in return for the destruction of Fort
Erie by the Americain. There were great
numbers of Indians in the town of the Sen-
eca nation, about 1000, who were come to
receive their annual allowance from the U.S.
about 6000 dollars — Some of them wer
fine athletic figures, many of them dressed
rudely enough to be sure but yet expen-

sively, their trousers being worked with
silk and silver thread. Their coats are
sometimes made as ours, and I think that
I could recognize the mortal remains of
several dandy coats upon the shoulders of
these primitive worthies.
Friday July 15. — Went out into the
woods which are in this vicinity, swampy
and impassable wildernesses — shot nothing
but a blue bird and several squirrells —
Passed some time with Mr. Salter a
brother of Mrs. Mappa's and much pleased
with him, & wrote to Mr. Mappa.
The Indians all drunk — one half
christian, the other pagan. —
Saturday July 16. At Eight A.M. set off
for Niagara, with a coach full of very
agreable company, crossed the St. Lawrence
where the stream runs at the rate of 10 mil[e]s
per hour — a beautiful and glorious river
and its waters clear as crystal. Passed
through the village of Chippewa, the vicin
ity of which was the scene of a conflict in
the last war between the Br. & American,

9[8]

forces. Long before our arrival
at this place, the noise of the waterfall
had become distinctly audible, and the
cloud of foam had been visible for an
equal distance. the coach drove up to
an elegant hotel (Forsyths) and in a
few minutes more I was at the falls.
I had thought and heard and read so
much of their sublimity, that at first
sight I was somewhat disappointed —
but I found that the longer I gazed upon
them, the more of sublimity became ap-
parent, and indeed by the time you have
looked steadily for a few moments, you became overpow[ere]d by the stupendous, the almighty scene. — The river is divided by an
island above the falls into two unequal
parts, the larger body of water falling on
the precipice on the Canadian side — for
1/2 mile above the falls the rapids begin
and there in themselves present a beautiful
spectacle; as the water, broken into a thousand cascades, rushes at the rate of 28 miles
per hour. — Then comes the mighty

cataract — the ridge of the precipice
taking into the account its curvature is
in extent more then 2000 feet, and on
some parts of the ledge the water is 20 feet
in depth — over the rock the water falls
from an elevation of 178 feet in the basin
which is one sheet of tumultuous foam,
and from and over it, the spray, like
a purely white cloud, rises in a thousand
fantastic shapes.  The top of the precipice
is formed of lime stone, for the depth of
about 6 feet — beneath this stratum the water
has worn away the slate rock, untill an
excavation of 30 or 40 feet in breadth has been
formed.  Into this cavern the adventurous
may enter, but I should be sorry to repeat
the experiment, as independently of the tremendous current of wind which almost
deprives you of breath, in one minute the
visitor will become wet through from the
spray. The descent to the bottom of the
falls may be performed two ways — 1st
by a spiral staircase, 2ly, by going
a few feet above the falls, and walking

100

into the stream, the waters of which
as they roll over the rock, would carry
any one down, without the least exertion
on his own part; this latter is not however
very frequently adopted, as the other is
generally supposed to be much safer.
There was a considerable number of visitors
at the falls, and so impressed was my mind
with the scene, that although much fatigued
with the personal labour and mental excitement of the day, I found it almost
impossible to sleep —
Sunday July 17th. Set off immed.y. after
breakfast with a Mr. Fuller — Mr. & Mrs. Myl-[?]
ra to the American side of the falls —
we crossed the river in a small boat, which
was however perfectly safe, and ascended the
other bank, an elevation of about 200 feet.
This division of the falls separated from
the other by goat island which is about
1/4 of a mile in extent, is about 700 or 800
feet in width, although from the other side
it appears but a trifling stream.
This fall separately considered is 10 times

larger than the Trenton falls, though it
contains less than 1/4 of the river. —
We crossed over a bridge to Goat island
and from a bridge which extends from its
banks over the rapids, had a splendid view
of the falls. From this point the scene
is perhaps the most imposing. — In the
afternoon set off for ~~Niagara, and~~
the town of Niagara about
15 miles distance, and passed thro' a
tolerably fertile and very well farmed
country — visited Brocks monument at Q.
Monday July 18.  Took the steam
boat Canada for York on the other
side of the lake — the distance is
36 miles — reached it in 4 1/2 hours
York is a thriving town contg.
5000 inhabs. it is rapidly increasing
and covers much ground. it is the
seat of government of U.C. and has a
very handsome Parliamt. House, which
is not however yet completed. —
Tuesday July 19th. Strolled about the
neighbourhood, and visited the government

offices where my enquiries were
answered with great civility, and here
I obtained the first authentic tidings of
R.P.H. who is Clerk of the Peace of
the district of Ultawa. lives at Hawkesbury. The musquitous very troublesome
Wednesday July 20th.  At 7 AM. as the
Gt.Britain S. Boat had unexpectedly
stopped at Niagara, took a berth
back to that place in order to proceed
in her down the river. —

The morg. fine but about 1/2 way
across the lake a heavy mist came in
which gradually condensed into the peculiar
clouds which are the forerunners of a squall
we immediately took in all sail and
prepared for a blow. — Interim a water
spout had formed within a short distance
of us, and all appearances presaged a
most violent storm. — Our attention
was diverted to a schooner at the distance
of 3/4 of a mile from us. I perceived
that there was no time for shorten[in]g sail
and watched her struck by the

squall with the most intense interest
The squall threw her on her beam end
and in 5 minutes she totally sunk. —
The storm had now reached us — and to
return to the wreck was impossible, as
for our own safety we were obliged to
head the wind — In an hour after
we tacked about and succeeded in pickg.
up 3 men — one of whom had swam
the whole time, one had been on the boat
which was turned upside down, another who
could not swim had rested on some spar.
There were six individuals drowned —
the Captain — a little boy, an Irishman
his wife — another passenger and one hand.
The last that was seen of the Captain
was when he was swimming with one
hand and supporting the child with the
other — such was the disastrous affair
We collected $24 for the 3 survivors
and landed them at Niagara. At 4 PM
the same day we set off in the Steam
Boat Great Britain — a fine and com-
modious boat

104

In our passage to Oswego, we sailed
over the spot where the schooner went down
but nothing save a few spars were visible
The Boat sailed rapidly along — 12 miles per
hour, and the line of the coast on the south
side furnished us with an ever varying scenery
The character of the shore is however very
tame. We passed Port Genessee and Toronto
Bay in the night and at 7 AM on
Thursday July 21rst. arrived at Oswego.
This pretty little town is situated on a river
of the same name, and a neat though
not a very spacious harbour is here constructed for the security of vessels. — There is a
branch canal here from the great Erie
Canal as it is called, and the salt made
at Salina is shipped in great quantities
here for the western countries. —
From Oswego proceeded across the lake
and entirely lost sight of land as the water
is here 60 miles across, but at length came
in view of some of the many island which
stud this end of the lace [i.e., lake]. At 4 PM we
reached Kingston, a large and thriving

town, where the military business of the
Upper Province is transacted — we stopped
here to take in some merchandize
and I had an hour for a ramble through
the town. — The scenery after leaving
Kingstown becomes most beautiful as
we enter the lake of 1000 islands. There are
in fact in this part of the river 1227
islands and rocks, all of them very picturesque, and though built of many stone
yet they have their summits clothed with
the most luxuriant foliage. — . . at about
9. PM we arrived at Brockville
a beautiful little town on the bank
of the river, and a rapidly increasing
place. — At 12 PM. we arrived at Pres-
cott, but by this time I was fast asleep
in my berth —
Friday July 22nd.  Breakfasted at a miserable hotel in the town and at 8 AM set
off in a stage for Cornwall — at this place
after being almost jolted to pieces we arrived
at 7 P.M. Our tribulations on the road
were however compensated for by the scenery

106

on the River — The island below
Brockville being larger and more fertile
than above, while the rapids of the river
breaking upon you at many a turn
add an interest to the scene —
In this town I first obtained intelligence
of my brother Phil as I supped at the
house where he had boarded for several years
Slept on board the steam boat that night
was nearly eaten up by vermin, but
what remained of me rose on the morning of the <u>Saturday July 23rd</u>
and found itself sailing away 12 miles an
hour down the river — We entered an ex-
pansion of the river called Lake St. Francis
a beautiful sheet of water, on the Americain
side of which stands St. Regis an Indian
village which forms as pretty an object
as an assemblage of mere huts can do.
While crossing the lake 3 Indians in
a canoe hailed the boat which stopped
while they paddled to it, to offer for
sale a fish which they had speared
it was a kind of pike, known

[107]

by the name of Muskinange, and is
considered a great delicacy — this pretty
little fish only weighed 40 lbs. The Indian
received a dollar for it, and a bottle of
rum, the contents of which disappeared
before they were 100 yards from the boat. —
we arrived at last at Les Cedres at which
place we landed, as the cascades com-
mence here — some of our party however
chose to hire a boat to go down them
an experiment which may be tried with
perfect safety if you take a pilot. —
We met once more at the Jnction of
the Ottawa with the St. Lawrence and embarked once more — There were at this
time 4 Steamboats in sight. the waters
of the Ottawa or Grand river are very dark
and I was far from pleased with their
mud colour — when seen in a tumbler
however it is perfectly transparent and de-
posits much less than the water of the St.
Lawrence — We crossed another Lake — that
of St. Louis where by the bye another singular
circumstance had taken place on the day of

108

the accident which happened on the
Lake Ontario — a shower having com
in two boys had taken shelter in a
coach which was on the deck of a Steamer
when a heavy squall of wind struck the vessel
and the wheels of the carriage not being secured
with the lurch of the boat, it gently glided
with its unlucky tenants into the bosom of
the deep. Fortunately it did not sink
directly, and the boys standing on the seats kept
their heads above the water in the confined body
of air contained in the roof of the coach
where they remained untill the boat was
lowered and they were taken out, when the
carriage immediately sunk. They were fishing
for it when we passed through the lake on
this day. — We arrived at Lachine at abt.
5 P.M. and took the stage to Montreal, where
I was truly delighted to rest my weary bones
— the evening wet and dirty, and so I went
to the theatre where the performance was
really exceedingly good.
Sunday July 24th. — No conveyance at
the Ottawa, so was obliged to sit down

contentedly there being no place of worship
of my own persuasion here. —
Montreal contains about 28000 inhabitants
and is a rapidly increasing place. The site
of the town is exceedingly favourable, but
the place itself is anything but attractive
The streets are exceedingly narrow, the houses
however are built of stone, but their many
iron doors and shutters give a gloomy and
unsocial appearance to the place. —
The number of Emigrants here is enormous
and a great deal of stress prevails amongst
them — custom however no doubt has rendered
their sufferings bearable, these sort of
things you know are nothing when you're
used to them. —
Monday July 25th. Returned to La Chine
and passed once more thro' the lake St.
Louis, and then commenced my voyage up
the Ottawa — (Mem.)(sang over the Canadian
boat song) after you become reconciled
to the colour of the water, the river is very
beautiful and when it expands into the
lovely sheet  of the lake of the 2 Mountains

110

forms with its surrounding shores a
most picturesque scene. — There is a
close succession of houses of each side
of the river and lakes — and a large Indian
village between the two lakes. There were
on the steam boat two of the Soeurs de
Charité who by the bye an English Lady
with what appeared to me an amazing degree
of cool impeudence (with reverence be it spoken
requested to sit down while she sketched their
costume &c. — These sisters were taken ashore
by some Indians in their canooe.
There is a pretty little Catholic chapel here
and there is one on the mountain which
forms a beautiful object as we sail up the
rive — The bulk of the population in
LC is catholic, and that body retains the
property which under the ancien regime
it possessed. In UC. there are both
Episcopalians Presbyterians Methodists &c.
and I was informed that there were Unitarians
sufficient in Montreal to support a place
of worship. — After passing thro' the lake of
the two mountains we came to the rapids

and there took a stage as no boat can
pass up the river. There is a noble canal
making here, in size and workmanship
infinitely superior to anything in the states
We travel about 10 miles in stage and
upon my arriving at Grenville, I
was glad to hear that I was only 3 miles
from my brother R.P.H. The captain of
the steam boat kindly sent his men with
me in a boat, and in another hour
I held in my arms a brother from whom
I had been separated 14 years —

My feelings upon the occasion can
be imagined much better than described
though it was anything but a common meeting. We had been separated for years, we had
parted in sorrow, clouds and darkness had been
been over and between, and we met in a land
some thousand of miles distant from our native
country, we again heard the familiar and
memoried voice, again beheld the well remem-
bered form and feature, altered indeed by age
and somewhat saddened by the influence of
sorrow, but our hearts were still the same

My sister in law and nephew were
then introduced to me, and I soon felt
myself at home.

Tuesday July 26th. — went out for the first
time in a canoe, and though I at first
found its management rather difficult
a little practice soon enabled to impel &
guide it with the small paddle. I spent
several hours amongst the island at the
head of the rapids. The Ottawa here expands
into a bay about 3 miles in width, presenting
a beautiful expanse of water bounded on
the north side by a range of hill about
400 or 500 feet in height. Beyond this elevation
the country is very mountainous, a complete
forest in fact, and the resort of wild animals
of every description. at the west end of the
bay the river contracts, and after being divided
by several islands shoots down some formidable rapids, which present an unsurmoun-
table obstacle to ~~cultivation~~ navigation.
The canal will however when finished avoid
the difficulty, and as the river for the next
60 miles is deep and tranquil,

it is destined to be a useful channel
for conveyance to and from the great mar
kets of Montreal and Quebec.
Wednesday July 27th. Took my gun into
the woods, but found very little game. I
passed through a prostrate forest which on
the 20th of last June, stood in all the beauty and pride of vegetation, a whirlwind on the
next day levelled 100 acres in less than five
minutes, to the great loss of the owner. —
Wild animals such as bears and wolves are
still plentiful in this part of the country, it
is only two years since a lynx crossed the
road very near to my sister who was walk
ing there, and a week or two since only
the wolves made sad havock in a flock
of sheep a few miles hence. — Some years
ago an old hunter crossed the bay in his
canoe, and not returning home was given
up as lost. A few weeks after his body
was found below the rapids clasping and
clasped in, the hug of a huge bear, which
had in all probability overturned his canoe
but perished in the revengeful and convul-

struggle of his unfortunate victim
A melancholy accident occurred in
May 1822 on or rather below the rapids
above mentioned. A Mr. Hamilton, an
enterprising and respectable gentleman who
has very extensive saw mills on the water
privilege lost 4 children in the following
manner. His wife and children were
crossing the river in a canoe at the foot of
the rapids, and their frail bark verging
too near to the agitated water, was overturned and its contents precipitated into the
river. 4 children were drowned and it was
supposed that the mother was lost also
untill an hour afterward as some one
turned up the canoe which had been
upset and in that position drawn on
shore, and found her, in a state of in
sensibility, with her arms convulsively
clasping the seats of the canoe. —
Wednesday July 27th. — Had a little
leisure to look about me and survey
the character of the country. There is
of course a great deal of wild land

in the vicinity — The soil is however
generally very good, and there appear to be
traces of iron are in the stones which
rather too plentifully cover the surface
of the ground in many places. —
These collections of large rounded stones
some of them many tons in weight
are a singular feature in the character of the country; they are generally
found on ridges or small elevations
while the flat ground is free from
them. — The population of this District of Ottawa amounts in number
to rather more than 4000 inhabs.
about 3 to a square mile — so that
there is yet sufficient room for emigrants. — There are in the neighbourhood several families of wealth and
respectability, and the character of
the people generally is very far from
bad. —
Thursday July 28th. In travelling thro
the woods I observe the immense
quantity of the white poplar, the

american tree of liberty, which
grows naturally on the soil of this
country. Wherever the fire has destroyed
a forest of the old growth, a new one of
this tree springs up, which is however valu
less. The large timber has all been
cleared away from this section of the
country, the Ottawa river providing
such facilities for its transportation to
market. —

Friday July 29th. Visited the village of
L'Oregnal 6 miles from Hawkesbury
in company with my brother. This village
is delightfully situated at one extremity
of a noble bay in this truly noble river
and is already an extensive settlement.
The Jail and Court House are here, the
former is however generally untenanted,
from this town is a pretty ride to an
elevation about 6 miles south, from
which a fine view is obtained of the
mountains to the north of the river
some of which are evidently of very
considerable elevation. —

Saturday July 30th. —
The number of Irish in the district is
very considerable, and no very friendly
feeling exists between them and the Cana-
dians. — The latter are a very peculiar
people. Their language is french or
rather a kind of Patois which is at
first even to a tolerable french scholar
very unintelligible. They are evidently
some years behind hand with the world
but the legislature are now taking steps
to secure the better education of the
people, district schools to the number
of 500 have been established in the two
provinces during the last 18 mo. and a
very general and powerful impulse appears
to have been given to the capacities and
energies of the people. —
Sunday July 31. Went over the bay
with several members of the family to
attend divine worship at Grenville, a
town of the north side of the river. —
The service was episcopal. the clergyman
receives 200£ per annum from government.

The service was well attended and
great order and interest appeared to prevail. This settlement formed at the
junction of the canal with the Ottawa
was called into existence by its being
a military station, and the resort of
the numerous labourers on the canal.
This public work presents an instance
of the somewhat culpable delay and expen-
diture which has hitherto I understand cha-
racterized many of the government operation
of this country.  Though only 13 miles in length
it has been 13 years without completion
and has already cost 700,000£ sterling. —
This canal must however necessarily have
been an expensive work, as it is cut thru
the solid rock and of a size sufficient to
allow of the passage of steamboats. —
from this point a very handsome steam
boat plies to Bigtown, a large and
thriving settlement at the junction of the
Rideau canal with the Ottawa, and from
the great communication has for several
years paid very well. —

Monday Augt. 1 —
Made up my mind to an expedition
and set off solus in a large canoe, with
the intention of visiting the Calumet, a
small but lofty waterfall on the north
bank of the river. The journey was longer and the fatigue much greater than
I had expected, and when within abt. 200
yards of the spot, the violence of the wind
and current carried me down so rapidly
that I narrowly escaped a journy down
the rapids themselves — while resting with
my canoe moored to the other side, and
reposing half asleep as in a cradle, I
was startled by something rushing thro
the woods, and taking up my rifle I
prepared to fire at the wild beast I
expected. when lo — an Indian a gen-
uine Indian tall gaunt and desolate
with his long black hair and warlike
sash stood before me. — I gave the
poor devil some brandy which he appeared to relish exceedingly — Mem. very
sorry I had not a tract to give him.

120
Tuesday Augt. 2nd
          A day very similar to those producing
the deluge, impossible to stir out of doors
thunder lightning rain clouds darkness
and storms — enough of August 2nd.
Wednesday — 3  By way of divertissement,
went a fishing caught a pike a pirch
and a cold. There is an abundance
of fish in the river of almost every
kind, and people may say what they
like, fishing where you have sport is
very pretty amusement; those who speak
of it illnaturedly, do so because they
have never had any luck. We all know
that the misanthropy of Dean Swift is
by many attributed to this cause, and it
is no doubt in the painful remembrance
of former days of piscatory disappointment
that he gave this witty and sarcastic
definition of a fishing rod — "A long stick
with a worm at one end and a fool at
the other." —
Thursday — 4  Again at the village of
L'Oregnal and made a few miles further

up the river to a french settlement
at the head of the bay before-mentioned
The view of the river is here exceedingly
beautiful. — The musquitous are nearly
disappeared. — by the bye these pretty little
creatures are very much slandered for I
have received little or no annoyance from
them during my sojourn in this country.
Friday — Spent in fishing &c
Saturday Augt. 6 — Ditto. —
Sunday Augt. 7th. — Again at church
12 minutes long an half a thought deep.
had a pleasant sail home
Monday Augt. 8th. — Again on the water
rowing my canoe about and singing
Ottawa tide thy trembling moon &c —
felt very romantic and happy. —
Tuesday Augt 9th. — Once more upon the
waters, and enjoyed for the last time
fishing &c. — How powerful in its
operation is that principle of the human
mind, which attaches us to objects as
well as persons. Now that I am
about to leave this place, its beau-

-tiful and varied scenery assures a
yet greater degree of interest. The expans
of water, the verdant field, the lofty
hill are regarded as friends, of whose
society you are soon to be deprived —
your communion with the spirits of the
place is about to be interrupted, other
scenes and other thought are about to
occupy your attention, and engage your
thoughts. If we thus regard the out
ward world — oh how much more deeply
must we be affected, when we part from
relations and friends — when we leave
them to encounter once more the chance
and the changes of time and space.
I am about to leave that Brother from
whom I have been so long separated
the mountain will again rise, the ocean
will again roll between us, and who
can tell if we shall ever meet again
in this world never — and in the world
to come — oh how dear how precious
in such a moment is the revelation of
a future and a better state, when those

who love shall never again be
severed and where the tears shall be
wiped from all eyes. —
Wednesday August 10th. — My brother
(who accompanies me part of the way)
and myself crossed the Ottawa
to Grenville, from which place we
took the stage to Point Fortune from
whence the steam boat leaves
for Lachine. — As we had to wait there
the whole evening, my brother took
me across the river to visit Judge
MacDonald — or as he is more generally called Big John. — This is one
of finest old men that I have ever
seen — as to face figure and disposition
he is a true nobleman. Having
been engaged as a North Wester for
many years, he has seen a great
deal of a savage life, and has under-
gone his share of hardships. He is
however a man of considerable reading
and great intelligence. — The river
which from Grenville to this place

124

is a succession of rapids is about
3/4 of a mile across — at about this place
every year when the ice breaks up, an
enormous bridge of ice forms across the
water, and sometimes accumulates to the
height of 40 or 50 feet. —
Thursday Augt. 11 — started at 6 AM for
Montreal — In passing down the river
I could not but again remark the exceeding beauty of the scenery — there was every
thing that could make the place interesting
wood water vally mountains, a clear blue
sky with here and there an eagle sailing
through the calm atmosphere. — We reached
Montreal at about 3. PM having travelled
all day at the rate of 10 miles an hour. —
In passing down Lac St. Louis I observed
again a singular mound of the southern
shore, which perfectly green and smooth
forms an odd contrast with the wood
and rocks by which it is surrounded. it
has the appearance of being artificial
but there are no records of its creation
either Indian or French.

Friday Augt. 12th.

Having passed a-
nother day in this disagreeable town, I
am forced to confess that it is not so much
so as I supposed. The weather being finer
and the streets cleaner than when I was
here before, all things wore a brighter as
pect. The greater number by far of the
inhabitants are Canadian and French is
the standard language of the place. The
Irish immigrants seldom meet with employment here, as the prejudice against
them runs very strong; their numbers
and appearance are appalling. We
crossed the St. Lawrence this evening 9
miles to La Prairie — a large village
on the south of the river and here I
parted from my Brother. — This is not
the place to dilate upon my feelings on
the occasion: their remembrance is trea-
sured up in my own heart. There let
it remain. We parted with the
expression of a hope that we might
meet again. Will it be so?

This evening I reached St. Johns
a pretty and thriving village on the River
Chambly the outlet of Lake Champlain. —
The distance from ~~St. Johns to~~ La Prairie
to this place is 19 miles. The road which
is absolutely atrocious lies throug a perfectly
flat country. The Chambly mountains at
a few miles distance, rising abruptly from
the plain to the height of 2000 feet form
a peculiar and interesting object, and of
these you retain a view from some distance
up the river. — St. Johns lies at the head
of some rapids which impede the navigation of the river. Its size is considerable, thoug by the side of the St. Lawrence
it is a mere rivulet. — As St. Johns is
the last halting place in the Canadas
I will here subjoin a few remarks
upon this interesting and important
section of the country. — Canada commences
about Lat. 42° its southern extremity resting
on Lake Erie — its south eastern boundaries
Ontario and St. Lawrence, ~~its eastern~~ & the 45th
degree Latt. . . its ~~south~~ east the state of

New Hampshire and New Brunswick
while to the north and north west its
extent is bounded only by a region of
almost eternal winter. — The area which
it encloses is some hundred million of acres
but its climate varies much less than might
be supposed in a country extending so many
degrees of l̸o̸n̸g̸i̸t̸u̸d̸e̸ latitude — Upper C.
except where is stretches away to the ̸e̸a̸s̸t̸
north of Lake Huron and the east of Lake
Superior, is generally a level country — .
The Lower Province is more mountainous
and both abound with an infinity of
Lakes and rivers — The land bordering on
Ontario and Erie is exceedingly fertile
and repays nobly for agricultural labour
it this portion of the Canadas which is
settling the most rapidly, and which from
year to year grows rapidly in wealth
and importance. The uncleared land in
this district sells at prices varying from
1 to 5 dollars per acre. — The Canada
company's land are partly here — though
their great tract lies upon the Lake

128

Huron. The inducements which have
been offered to purchasers in this part have
had the effect of drawing immense numbers
of capitali[s]ts and labourers — and general
prosperity seems to await them all. —
The plan adopted by the Legislature of selling
untenanted lands for taxes due upon them
has given a great stimulus to the attention
and exertions of owners, and though in some
cases, the law may have fallen very hard
in its operation, there is no doubt but what
it has produced much good. The pr[o]ductions
of lower Canada are very similar, though upon the whole the soil is not of so good a
quality, but it is happy for both provinces
that agriculture is more generally and scien-
tifically pursued than it has hitherto been. —
The lumber trade, which has been of so
much consequence to the country is not
so great a favourite as it has been; it
is true that it occasionally makes a man
rich but it is not less certain that it
very often makes them poor, and to fol-
low it with any hopes of success requires

so much personal exertion and suff-
ering on the part of those concerned in
it that the number and respectability
of its followers is rapidly diminishing.
The agricultural produce which I observed
appears to me particularly healthy and strong
though it had not certainly that richness ø f
and luxuriance which characterizes the
United States. — The valuable timber is
cut away almost entirely from the land
easily accessible, and lumber merchants
have now to travel very far into the woods
before they can fix their shanties. It is
perhaps fortunate for the provinces that fires
in the woods are so much more rare
than in the States. The land is thus less
impoverished, and the timber allowed to at-
tain a respectable growth. — A tremendous
fire occurred however about 30 Years since, which
ravaged a large portion of country, and near
the banks of the Ottawa about Hawkesbury
the lofty skeletons of once noble trees, yet
remaining, contrast singularly with the thick
and luxuriant vegetation beneath them

[134]
Saturday Augt. 13th. This morning we left
St. Johns in a handsome Seamboat and
commenced our voyage up the river Chambly. — There is nothing very interesting abt.
this water untill you come to the lake
Champlain, which besides being a beautiful
sheet of water in itself, is interesting from
the transactions which took place upon it
during the late war. — The various sites of
forts and defences — the situation of the
fleets at the time of action, all pointed
out in the very useful guide books, render
this voyage a very lively one. Some of the
islands are very beautiful, and the deep and
frequent indentations of the lake into the shore
make this piece of water much more interes
ting than the large lakes. At Crown Point
the lake once more contracts into a river
and by the time you reach Whitehall there
is scarcely room enough for the steamboat
to turn. — There is some fine scenery on
this part of the river, the rocks are exceedingly
high and abrupt, and every now & then the

eye sees through the narrow openings the
lofty and distant summits of mountains.
Sunday Augt. 14th. — left at 8 AM for
Albany in a stage, the day very sun-
ny and hot. Our road lay through a
mountainous country the elevations known
by the name of the Green mountains
being to our left. — some of them I should
judge to be at least 3000 feet high, probably more. Their forms are much varied
The valleys between them are generally settled
and the rapid streams afford an abundance
of Mill seats. Salem Cambridge Troy
were the principal places through which
we past on this route. The latter place
is rapidly increasing, but I believe
principally celebrated for the manufacture
of coaches, which are sent from thence to
all parts of the U.S. —         The stage in
which we travelled was most diabolically
horsed, and our last change of cattle had
been treated for the last 5 weeks in the
following manner, driven 38 miles per
driver three days in the week & 19 three more

Their condition may be more easily
imagined than described. At last we
reached Albany, where having been once
before, I felt myself comparatively at home
I was however ill — very ill.
Monday Augt. 15th. Perambulated the
town to my great satisfaction, as it
was very full of girls, and is I
believe much celebrated for them. — I engaged
a birth in the steam boat for N.Y. and at
3 P.M. set off after having been annoyed
by the runners till I lost all patience.
The following is a specimen of a dialogue
between myself and one of them

R.    Going to Phila. Sir?

H.    I am.

R.    Won't you go by the "New Phila. boat Sir

H.    No.

R.    It is a fine boat, a great many people
      go in it.

H.    The very reason I do not. I do not
      like to be bothered by many or one

R.    Your going by the "[blank]" I guess

H.     If it is any business of yours I
am. If not as I suspect, once for
all go about your business, or in another moment I will make an example of you;

After being detained by runs ashore, we pro
ceeded down the river, but when night
came, such was the crowded state of the
the boat and so intense was the heat, that it
was impossible to remain below, and I
passed all night upon the deck. — Most glad
was I when the dawn of the morning brot.
us to N.Y.

Tuesday Augt. 16th. — Remained at N.Y.
all day — too ill to travell

Wednesday Augt. 17th. Set off for Pa. at
7 A.M. had the vexation of remaining 3
hours aground in the Raritan — when we
reached Trenton N.J. the Steam boat had
left us; we were obliged to remain there
all night. It was a day of disagreeables
There was however a cheerful company of
us and about 8 of us passed the time merrily
enough. —

138

Thursday Augt. 18th.

Reached Pa. after having been absent
two months. My letters were of consequence
of such a tenor that I found it would
be requisite to return home. I had however
to visit the Pocono once more. But
I was seriously ill and found myself
obliged to undergo the prescribed of bleeding
blistering, fasting &c and I was a
prisoner untill the
Augt 29th. when I travelled from Pa.
to Easton. There is nothing at all interesting on this route, and of the town itself I
have previously given you a sketch. —
Thursday Augt. 30th. Took a long walk up
the banks of the Delaware, the attractions
of which had much increased since I last
visited the scene — the foliage of the trees
was now in its luxuriance and highest splendour, before the least autumnal change
had taken place; how many a time did
I exclaim "beautiful beautiful" and indeed
in the spirit of that principle by which we
only know how to value, when we

are about to lose, the conviction
that, in all human probability I should
behold these scenes no more, added a deeper
interest and a more witching charm to
them. —
Wednesday Augt. 31.  Set off at 3 AM
for the Pocono — I pass over the account
of this journey, more rapidly than I did
over the road, for there was nothing to
interest me; It may be that I have
not a very creative imagination, or con-
templative mind, or I should perhaps have
found poetry in half a dozen little mill
        food for meditation in
streams, or ∧ a thousand solemn forests which
we passed, but I am "aweary" of making
up thoughts and feelings, it is an unprofitable kind of manufacture, producing nothing
but very flimsy articles. The surveyor who
accompanied me, and myself arrived at
the Pocono about mid-day having travelled
at the rate of 3 1/4 miles per hour, a pace
which however much it may secure from
outward danger is too decidedly productive
of feelings of impatience and thoughts of
                      suicide

In the afternoon of this day we went
on a fishing excursion down the Mud Run
and caught a few trout, which we found an
agreable addition to our supper and our breakfast next morning. —
Thursday Sept. 1rst. On this day had my
health been good I should have sailed from
America, but instead of that, here I am, in
the midst of this interminable wilderness. —
Our route this day, lay about 12 miles thro'
the woods, to walk which distance under
such circumstances is an employment by
no means a sinecure. We took our
guns with us, and shot a few wild pigeons
When about 6 miles from home, the
rain began to fall and continued to
annoy us. It was impossible to return
home without getting thoroughly wet, which
we accordingly did, nor was there any
other resource for us the remainder of the
day but to smoke cigars &c. —
Friday Sept. 2. Rain Rain Rain —
set off at 1 P.M. for Wilkesbarre a place
which I was very anxious to see, as it

is situated in the valley of "Wyoming"
which has been the scene of so much blood-
shed, and has been rendered yet more interesting by Campbells poem of Gertrude of
Wyoming. The road to this place lies
over the broad mountain, which extends
30 miles; the route is very bad, the
bottom of the road being what they call
"corduroy", but as a fellow passenger observed by no means velvet. This range of
hills contains some of the wildest country which I have ever passed through;
there are but few houses along the road, and
and [sic] one unvarying forest meets the eye on
every side. Several creeks cross the road
and a̶t̶ where the Lehigh traverses it,
there was some years since a flourishing
town called "Stoddartsville" — it is now in
ruins, and forms a melancholy object, too
much in unison with the wilderness which
surrounds it. — Before we began to descend
the mountain, the evening closed in upon us
and the rain which had been pouring in
torrents during the day, rendered the night

of a yet more pitchy darkness
The descent of the mounn. is very precipitous, and by no means agreable.
The view of the valley from the summit of the last hill is exceedingly beautiful, and is perhaps unequalled in America.    At last we reached the bottom
and the horn of the coachman sounded
forth in accents perfectly excruciating,
and truly eloquent of the misery of the
passengers, the intelligence that we
were near — Inn — supper bed and all
that sort of thing ensued of course. —
Saturday Sept. 3rd.  The day fine and
the appearance of the valley truly beautiful.
In the morning I strolled southward
over a fine country through which the
Susquehanna, here about 600 feet wide,
winds its beautiful course. — In the
afternoon I visited the coal mines
about 2 miles to the N.E. — The
anthracite coal is of a very valuable
kind, but the mine is not at present worked to a very great ex-

tent. There are some other mines
about 5 miles to the south, much
more prosperous and extensive. —
The day went down in grandeur. The glory of the autumnal sunset filled the sky
and shed a thousand lines of beauty upon
earths varied scenery.
Sunday Sept. 4th. The whole of the valley enveloped in mist, but the morning
sun at last cleared the atmosphere, &
as there was no U. place of worship in
the town, and the day was so very temp-
ting I determined to take a ride up the
valley, to the "Narrows," where the river
breaks thro the mountains into the vale
of Wyoming. After crossing the western side of the river, you take a norther-
ly direction, and pass very near to the
foot of the western mountains which bound
the vale. In following this course, you
pass by and over the scene of many
interesting events. — The rock on which
19 whites were murdered and scalped is
still remaining in its original position.

144

and credulity still points out a
few veins of iron coloured stone upon
the surface, as the stains of the victims
blood. — Very near to this the merciless
destruction of a brother by a tory took
place. It was on a small island
in the river, where the unfortunate fella
after throwing away his rifle, had con-
cealed himself in the grass and logs.
Discovered by his brother, he came from
his place of concealment, and throwing
himself on his knees begged for mercy
and offered to be his brother's slave for life.
That may be all very well, said the tory
but you are a d—d rebel, and shot
him thro the head. — About 2 miles
above this the battle took place between
the Americains under Coll. L. Butler
and the British and Indians under
Colls. J. Butler and Brandt. — the par-
ticulars of this bloody affray and still more
bloody massacre are too well known to
need repetition here. And the pen of
Campbell, has given an additional

interest to these scenes and circumstances which cannot die. — The nature
and situation of the valley are
altogether so beauteous and advantageous
that it may well have been the object
of so much contest between the different
tribes of Indians — and subsequently the
Connecticut and the Pensylvanian settlers.
There are in this valley also, remains
of fortifications, similar to those in the
western country which indicate the
residence of a people far superior to the
Indians themselves. It is unaccounta-
bly strange that there should be no
explanatory tradition amongst the
savage tribes, but all remains in dark
ness. — A few miles higher up the scenery
of the gap is very splendid, and though
far inferior in grandeur to that of the
Delaware water Gap, has a degree of
beauty which amply repays you for the
visit. —
Monday Sep. 5th. This day was spent
in fishing in the river and the adjacent

146

ponds which abound with pike
and yellow perch. — The town of
Wilkesbarre contains about 1200 inhabitants, and though not at present very
rapidly increasing, will at some future
day doubtless contain a much greater
number of residents. The inhabitants
of the valley are of very mixed origin
German Dutch Yankee, English Irish
&c. but original distinctions are very
wisely forgotten, and the fellow feeling
of citizenship appears to prevail, to the
exclusion of minor distinctions. —
Tuesday Sep. 6th. Visited the Plymouth
mines this morning, which are of very
considerable extent, the opening to them
lying in a small ravine on the west
side of the river. — This coal is anthracite, and the bed is of very great thickness
and there appears reason to believe that
the supply in this neighbour[hoo]d is fairly
inexhaustible. — There are some beautiful remains of vegetable found a-
mong the coal and the neighbouring

slate. It is a singular fact t̶h̶a̶t̶
in relation to this valley, that while the
banks of the Susquehanna both above &
below have been for the last 10 years very
unhealthy particularly in the autumn, this
chosen spot has been spared from the
epidemic diseases common to the country
in its vicinity.

I could not but think as I looked
upon the beautiful and placid vale, studded
with the abodes of peace and industry, and
cultivated like a garden, by the hands of the
husbandman, of the mighty change that the
progress of a few years had made. Where
formerly a warlike race, now only known by
the ruins of their fortifications once dwelt,
where subsequently, where subsequently the ruder
Indian-tribes dwelt and fought and died,
where still later the white men became each
other's murderers, that spot so favoured by
all that nature can confer, is now the happier home of plenty peace and tranquillity
All these changes and a thousd. more have
taken place, and the same sun shines

and the same sweet stream flows along
and the "eternal hills" remain, the same
yesterday to-day and for ever. — Oh how
transient is this individual existence, when even race after
race has past away, and nation succeeded to
nation, the tenants of an unchanging world.

It was with no small degree of regret
that I prepared to leave the valley of Wyoming
and I would most gladly have remained
much longer, had not the pressure of business
prevented me. —
Thursday Sep. 7.  At 4 A.M. the coach
started from the Inn, and the unfortunate
equipage had to make its way thro' a drizzling
rain, and a dark uncomfortable morning,
but as the morning light advanced into day,
the new beauties which continually disclosed
themselves, reconciled me to that day's journey. My companions in the coach were
very agreable. We passed thro' Berwick
& Danville, two small but rich towns and
late in the evening arrived at Northumberland.
Friday Sep. 8th.  Left this place at day-
break, and had light enough to enable

us to appreciate the extreme beauty of
its situation. It is built at the junction
of the north and west branches of the Sus-
quehannah, which for half a mile below
expands into a broad beautiful and tranquil
basin at the other side of which Sunbury
appears to great advantage; The banks of
the river still retain their hilly character
but every now and then a flat intervenes
which is of courn cultivated. On our arrival
at Liverpool, we left the coach and were ferried
over the river which is here 3/4 mile wide
shallow and very rapid. We proceeded over
most villainous roads, and ascended a hill
at an elevation of 900 feet above the river
and from the top of which there is a very
beautiful though bounded prospect. In
descending we obtained a view of the State
house at Harrisburg, overtopping the interminable foliage, and forming a beautiful
object through the vista of the mountains.

The conversation of the passengers happened to turn upon the subject of slavery
and I was astonished to find, such a

150

complete absence of moral feeling as was
displayed by some of them. One young
lady, a Southron in particular, spoke in
a manner which both shocked and disgus-
ted me. —    At last we reached Harrisburg, a pretty systematically built town
containing about 4000 inhab.  This place
is the seat of the government of the state
and the building devoted to their service is
a very handsome one. —

I was sorry to be under the necessity of remaining at this place another
day, on account of the disease which was
so universally prevalent. Fever and Ague
Bilious Fever, Typhus Fever, had their different victims in almost every house, and
at the Inn where I put up, there were
no less that six seriously ill with either
the one complaint or the other. It is
difficult to account for the prevalence of
illness in this section of the country, for
the Susqua. is very rapid here, and the
illness made its appearance before the con-
struction of the canals, though very

many attribute this misfortune to
the water which necessarily stagnates in
them.

Sunday. Set off from Harrisg. in a
full stage, the day exceedingly hot, the
roads very bad, the country uninteresting
the passengers vulgar. I record this day
as one of the most miserable in my
life time, so much so that the mere
remembrance of its various evils well
nigh distracts me. —          In entering
Maryland which is a slave state, we
met great quantities of Negroes. They appeared very happy, and insensible to the
vulgar gibes and unmanly insults of the
stage passengers, who indulged the pro
pensity to insult the unfortunate, at
the expense of these injured people. —

There must, there will be an end
to this before long, the system of slavery
which began in villainy, and which has
been continued in tyranny, will end in
destruction. There are now upwards of
2,000,000 slaves in the U.S. and

152

when they [k]now their power, and
have learned to concentrate their force
may God have mercy on their op-
pressors.     I know that the question
of their emancipation, brings along with
it many obstacles, it is natural that it
should be thus: it is the heaviest pen-
alty of crime where in the moral the social or the political world, that it is
difficult to return to virtue, but some
means must be put in action to lessen
the danger arising from the existence of
such an immense body of men, whose
interests are different from the community
amongst which they live, and who are set
apart from the tyranny and the scorn of
those who happen to have a white skin.

        The late insurrection in Virginia though
on a small scale indicates the measures
to which th[e]y will eventually resort. —

        At last I reached Baltimore complete[l]y
exhausted, and glad to retire to rest. —
Monday Sep. 12.  After some
little trouble, discovered Mrs. B

residence. She was much pleased
to see me, and welcomed me kindly
ro her house. Baltimore is a large
and rapidly increasing coml. city.
Containg. a popn. of more than 80,000
it has risen through all the mutations
and ¢h∉n∉∉∉ reverses of fortune to the fourth station amongst Americain cities.
The splendid bay of the Chesapeake fur-
nishes an admirable sea communication, whilst the great Susquehanna
pours down the produce of one half of
Pensylvania. The churches and public
buildings are numerous and prospering.
The monument to Washington is one
of the most splendid in the country
and there is one upon a smaller scale
to the memory of the soldiers who
fell at North West Point. The
view of the bay from Federal Hill
and the summit of the first mentioned mont. is most splendid the
waters of the bay being covered with
shipping. Left for Washington

154

Tuesday Sep. 13th. —
Of all the dismal rides that I
ever experienced, that from B. to
W. is the worst. — The country is
barren and perfectly unlovely. —
A great part of it has been cleared,
and 200 years ago, this district of
country was thickly inhabited. The
soil naturally barren, has been still
further impoverished by unremitting
cultivation, and the growth of tobacco
that dear delightful but noxious weed
has exhausted it so much that a
little poor grass is at present the
only vegetation upon it. — Here and
there however you meet with a
field of tobacco ánd or corn.
Washington, the seat of government
of an extensive important and spi-
rited empire, is unworthy of its
enviable distinction. There is nothing in this city (setting aside the
capitol and the President's house)
which at all meets the expectation

of a stranger — The number of
the inhab. is abt. 19,000 exclusive
of George Town which is separated from it by t̶h̶e̶ Rock Creek.
Both are one the Potomac a noble sheet of water. There is howev[er]
little or no shipping here, and the
whole surrounding country is a desert.

The President's house is a handsome building much in the English
style of a county seat of a noble
and the Capitol is an edifice, the
beauty and indeed grandeur of which
would reflect honour upon any
country. — The length of the building
is 358 feet, its height 180, a large
dome surmounts the centre, w̶h̶i̶c̶h̶
the top of which there is a
truly noble view, diminished in
effect only by the barrenness of
the immediate vicinity.

Not much company here at present, Winter being the time for
the assembly of Congress. —

[156]
Back to Baltimore. No time
for remaining any where now. —
Now that I am to return, my
impatience to see once more
my country and those I love ex
ceeds all bounds — Oh how the spirit
burst through all impediments of
times and space and sees and hears
the objects of its love. —
Wed. Sep. 14.  Yesterday I thought
nothing on earth could have kept
me in B. another day; the per-
suasive voice of a woman has
induced to remain. — Went on the
Baltimore and Ohio road as far
as Ellicott's mills 13 mil[e]s. — Our
[carriage] containg. abt. 15 passengers was
drawn by one horse at the rate
of 10 m. per hour. The steam
engine which has been put on
this route has not answered the
expectation of the projectors, and is
now undergoing alteration. —
        The work upon some parts

of this route to the mills has
been immense. — Solid rock has
been cut through to the depth of
70 feet, and other excavations
of 80 & 85 feet have been made.
When finished it will be a noble
work. Observe that I say when
finished, for its intended course
cannot be less than 350 miles
and may be more. — The rails
are all imported from England, as
not withstanding the various expen-
ses incurred, they can be procured
at 40 dollars per ton less from
this source, than from home manufacture. — there is some very
beautiful scenery on the latter
part of the road.The Tarpeian
Rock, by the rail road classics
called Terrapin, is a bold precipice
and hill and ravine, and forest
rock and cottage, and the rapids
and falls of the Patahsco, are mingled
in delightful confusion. —

158
Thursday Sep. 15th. —
Goodbye Baltimore, goodbye
Miss B. goodbye Maryland,
a state so free, that a man may
sell his own slave, — happy
happy land. — Sailed d̸o̸w̸n̸ along the bay
at 10 m. the hour, in a noble
steamboat, t̸o̸o̸k̸ passed into the
great canal, which unites the
Chesapeake with the Delaware.
This canal is spoken of by the Ams.
with great pride and it is certainly a
very considerable work. — The excavation
is in some parts very deep, and the width
of the canal very considerable. So much
stagnant water however lies in the extensive hollows thro which it passes, that
the neighbouring country must be exceedingly unhealthy. I observed a very
singular plan adopted, to secure the
high banks, which as they are of a very
loose soil, would be liable to be washed
into the canal in heavy rains, that of
thatching them in the same manner

as our English cottage roofs are
formed. Opposite to the spot where
this canal joins the Delaware, there
is a low island in the very centre of
this noble river, on which is situated a
fort. The position though low is very
commanding, but the fort itself both
badly constructed, and a good deal neglected also. — The evening became very
stormy, and I was not sorry to beholed
once more the wharves at Philadela.

Immediately upon landing I
secured a birth in the Algonquin, Cap.
W. West, and then reached once more
the hotel which I had previously made
my home. —
Friday 16.
Satury. 17    Were employed in vis-
Sunday 18    iting and taking leave
Monday 19   of my friends at Pa.
amongst whom I make a mem of
the following — Miss Wilson, Swander
Harrold, Merrill Furniss Taylor Vaughan, Cadbury

160

Tuesday Sep. 20th. —
After having taken leave of a̶ f̶e̶w̶
my friends I embarked on board a
Steamboat, which was to convey us to
the Algonquin, she having gone down
with the preceding tide. As the wind
was then contrary, we took the captains
gig and paid a visit to a small town,
known by the name of Delaware City.

What this place may become at some
future day I know not, but it certainly
is not much like a city now, the whole
population not amounting to more than
200 or 300 souls. — We returned by
the light of the full moon, the last which
was to shine upon my sojourn in America
and the anchor being weighed that night
the next day we left the capes of May
Henlopen and —
M̶o̶n̶d̶a̶y̶ Wednes Sept. 21. We were once more
at sea. — Our voyage for the first few
days advanced but slowly, as light
and baffling winds prevailed, but
on the Sunday a westerly wind

sprung up, which continued during
the remainder of the voyage. — and after the usual alternations of wet and
dry weather, and the more than unu-
sual motion of the vessell, we arrived
at Liverpool on Friday [October] the 14th Inst.

Our passage up the Irish channel
was delightful as we there got into much
smoother water, the welch mountains
the noble rocks of Holyhead, and the verdure
of the earth after a three weeks absence
from its cheering view, and above all
the consciousness that I was fast approaching a reunion with the friends whom
I most love, filled my mind with the
most pleasing emotions. A Steamer
came alongside. I bid adieu to
the Algonquin and to all my companions save one, a Mr. Smith of Reddish
House. Mr. Stockpost who accompanied
me to the Star & Garter Hotel, where
I met once more, with something like
that comfort, which had so long been
denied to me. —

Now that I am returned, let
me note a few reflexions upon my
journey and the land which I have
visited. America, considered with respect to her physical qualifications, is
certainly a noble country. No where perhaps in the universe, could a land be
found comprising so many natural ad-
vantages. Her extent of latitude gives
her almost every variety of climate, her
soil is productive almost beyond any
other portion of the globe, her intermi
nable forests afford the beauty of foliage
and the utility of the most valuable timber, her extensive lakes and gigantic
rivers supply ample means for internal communication.

The history of her settlement
by an European population is too well
known to need any remark from me,
it will be worth while however to name
that, generally speaking, the Americains
have a nationality of character in as
great a degree, as the inhabitants of any

other, and exhibit traits of peculiarity
which cannot be found elsewhere. —
From whatever country emigrants
may come, they seldom ̸r̸e̸t̸a̸i̸n̸ trans-
mit their national characteristics
either physical or moral, further than
one generation. Dutch French English
Spanish Scotch Irish Swiss, all merge into
the Americain. The Dutch however apr.
to me to retain their peculy. the longest

*for remainder of observations see the
Lectures. —

Saturday Sep. [i.e., Oct.] 15th. After having eagerly de
voured all the news, and lamented over
the rejection of the Reform Bill, which
had just taken place, I left Liverpl.
and travelled on the Rail Road to Manchester, and from thence the same evening
to Derby, a place which I longed to re
visit, endeared as it was by a thousand
interesting recollections.

In passing thro' Ashbourne I enquired
after several of my old acquaintance, to the
two first enquiries I received the answer of
Dead Dead. What a change does the lapse
of a few years effect. A few years more
perhaps and he who will ask for me, will be
told in like manner that I am dead. —

I reached Derby late at night and
in the morning called upon my old acqain
tance and friends, who were all glad to see
me and to renew the communion which so
many years had been interrupted. It must
be at least six years since I was at this place

How all things are changed, the old dead
the young grown old, &c. —
Monday $\cancel{Sep}$. Oct. 17.  Visited Nottn. my
native town & spent 2 days with the
Spencers, who most hospitably entertained
me. I saw the Redfearns also
changed for the worse. The castle was
in ruins having been burned by the
mob a few days previous. —
Wednesday $\cancel{Sep}$. Oct. 19.

Left Derby by the

Mail for London and reached Brn.
once more at 3. Oclock Thursday
P.M.
Friday $⌀⌀. Oct 21.  Occupied in writing
letters and on Saturday commenced once
more the discharge of my ordinary duties. —
        Nothing particular occurred untill
Friday Nov. 25th. when I sent a letter
to Phil
Saturday Nov. 26.  After retiring to rest
at night was awoke by a violent attack
of the Pleurisy, which nearly brought me
to the grave. After losing abt. 120 oz of blood
the inflammation was subdued, and on the
Friday I was considered out of Danger. —
        I wish here to note down a record of
what my feelings were, in the immediate
prospect of dissolution. —
        With respect to my religious faith I
was perfectly at ease, believing Unitarianism
to be Christianity, and convinced that whether
it were or were not, a mere belief is of
no consequence in either meriting God's favor
or displeasure. With respect to my past

166

life, the remembrance of many and
late offenses lay heavily upon my mind.
I did not however feel that inclination to cry
for mercy mercy, but rather a disposition
to submit resignedly and cheerfully to whatever punishment my Heavenly Father should
see fit to inflict upon me. — A confidence
deep and unwavering, in Gods goodness, wisdom and mercy, never I believe forsook me
and in the conviction that all his ways are
and must be, the kindest wisest and the
best, I felt prepared to submit to what was
required of me, and "resigned to die or resolute
to live["?], left all to God. —
Saturday Decr. 10th. Now that I am fast
recovering, let me endeavor to draw a useful
lesson from the past. —

    For month after month, my illness
instead of diminishing appeared to settle
into a settled disposition to decline —
The harassing cough symptomatic of this
disease, tormented me continually, and
prevented me from taking the nourishment
requisite for the recovery of my strength.
in the beginning of March, a confirmed
affection of the lungs displayed itself
in loss of voice and inflammation —
Bed Bleeding blistering and all that sort
of thing for a fortnight. — It is here
worthy of remark that my Brother in
law never once came to visit me during
my illness, while from my sisters and
from I[.] Rogers I experienced the most
unvarying kindness and attention. —
    After I left my room, my
nerves were in such a shattered state
that I could almost have fancied the
approach of actual derangement, a total
loss of nightly rest distressed and weakened
me — and so pressing did the sense of
distraction become, that some relief

from business was absolutely essential.

[Prayer tucked into cover]


Great God whose lovliest name is Love
    (So Jesus tells me)
Look down from thy bright Heaven above
    On all who come to thee

When sin or grief or care assail
    Oh may my bosom still
Lean on that rock which cannot fail
    And bow before thy will. —

Jesus hath taught me to resign
    Unto thy will mine own
"Father, <u>thy</u> gracious will, <u>not mine</u>
    For evermore be done."

To this my griefs and cares I'll bring,
    Lay d̸o̸w̸n̸ at thy feet my woes
And seek beneath thy shadowy wing,
    With christ a f̸o̸n̸ sweet repose.

1. Hudson River

2. Mount Auburn Cemetery

3. Easton

4. Baltimore

5. Saw Mill, Delaware

6. Delaware River

7. Philadelphia Water Works, Schuykill River

Independence Hall
Philadelphia
originally the State
House, built 1732

8. Independence Hall, Philadelphia,
   originally the State House, built 1732

Christ Church, Philadelphia

9. Christ Church, Philadelphia

New York, Hudson River

10. New York, Hudson River

Near Baltimore

11. Near Baltimore

12. Genesee [River], Rochester [with Aqueduct Bridge]

13. Genesee River in Rochester

14. Rochester

15. Lower Falls, Rochester

16. Middle Falls, Rochester

17. Rochester Tannery

18. Kempshall's Mills, Rochester

19. Baltimore & Ohio Railroad

20. Montreal

Burned Forest near Ottawa

21. Burned Forest near Ottawa

22. British Fort at Niagara

23. Queenstown

24. Niagara River

25. Canadian Falls

26.  American Fall

27. Capitol, Washington

28. Gerards Bank, Phila.

29. Albany

The Monument, Baltimore

30. The Monument, Baltimore